Assessment and the
secondary school teacher

Assessment and the secondary school teacher

H. G. Macintosh
Secretary
Southern Regional Examinations Board

in collaboration with

D. E. Hale
Deputy Secretary
Southern Regional Examinations Board

Routledge & Kegan Paul
London, Henley and Boston

First published in 1976
by Routledge & Kegan Paul Ltd
39 Store Street,
London WC1E 7DD,
Broadway House,
Newtown Road,
Henley-on-Thames,
Oxon RG9 1EN and
9 Park Street,
Boston, Mass. 02108, USA
Set in IBM Press Roman by
Express Litho Service (Oxford)
and printed in Great Britain by
Unwin Bros. Ltd.

ISBN 0 7100 8472 2 (c)
ISBN 0 7100 8473 0 (p)

The Students Library of Education has been designed to meet the needs of students of Education at Colleges of Education and at University Institutes and Departments. It will also be valuable for practising teachers and educationists. The series takes full account of the latest developments in teacher-training and of new methods and approaches in education. Separate volumes will provide authoritative and up-to-date accounts of the topics within the major fields of sociology, philosophy and history of education, educational psychology, and method. Care has been taken that specialist topics are treated lucidly and usefully for the non-specialist reader. Altogether, the Students Library of Education will provide a comprehensive introduction and guide to anyone concerned with the study of education, and with educational theory and practice.

Contents

Contents

Acknowledgments

The authors would like to acknowledge the considerable help they received from many teachers working within the region of the Southern Regional Examinations Board in the preparation of this book. They would also like to thank their colleagues at the SREB, especially Mr K. Kenyon, for much fruitful discussion and Ormond Tate of the Curriculum Division of the New Zealand Department of Education for a helpful critique of the manuscript in draft. The work of developing and improving assessment practice as this book emphasises is a co-operative venture and the authors are very grateful to the following individuals and bodies for granting permission to reproduce material: Mr D. Drew; Dr J. Duffey; Professor R. L. Ebel; Mr J. Miller; Educational Testing Service, Princeton, New Jersey; the Joint Matriculation Board; the Meadway School; the Middlesex Regional Examinations Board; the New Zealand Department of Education; the Southern Regional Examinations Board and the University of London School Examinations Council.

The always tedious task of deciphering the manuscript and reducing it to proper order has been carried out with their usual cheerfulness and efficiency by Mrs S. M. Harris and Mrs M. E. Waldman.

Introduction

Any book about assessment ought at the outset to face up to the question 'Why assess?' There has in recent years been increasing concern about the effects of assessments upon the individual, and there is a school of thought that abhors the competition and social divisiveness which they consider result inevitably from assessment. Assessment is thus regarded as being degrading to both assessor and assessed. In the authors' opinion this point of view stems from a confusion between the act of assessment and the use to which the results of that assessment are subsequently put. There are first of all individual reasons which overwhelmingly justify the continuance of assessment. Young people and their parents need counselling in respect of their personal development and guidance in relation to their future careers. Whoever provides this help, it must, if it is to be of use, be based upon information collected as accurately and comprehensively as possible about the individual's abilities, potential, interests and personality. During a crucial period of any young person's life a key source of such information is likely to be his or her teacher and it is inevitable that much of what is obtained from this source will concern attainment.

Many would also argue that there are social reasons which justify the continuance of assessment. Even in a totally comprehensive education system there is need to make judgments among and about individuals and hence to evaluate. To evaluate is to appraise or determine the value of. It thus involves an estimation of worth and a quantitative comparison of values and these are essential elements in assessment. Teaching itself is impossible without evaluation. Every time a question is asked, every time a response is made, evaluation and hence assessment takes place. The authors would contend, therefore, that the question 'Why assess?' is the wrong question. We ought instead to be asking 'How can we assess more effectively in order that the information we gather is more likely to be of use for the purposes we have in mind?'

Teachers in secondary schools, the area with which this book is concerned, have in the past been placed in a very restricted position in relation to assessment. Their principal shackle has been the external examination. This has not only inhibited their ability to develop courses of study appropriate to the needs of their pupils but has also restricted their view of assessment because of the limited uses to which the results of external examinations are put. Grading and selection have been the primary functions of external examinations although there has also been an element of prediction within the process of selection. The comparatively limited range of assessment techniques employed in external examinations has, moreover, not been helpful because it has discouraged experimentation in teaching by rewarding too highly those who gear their teaching methods to the techniques used. One obvious solution is to abolish external examinations; a second would be to involve the teacher more directly in their control. In Britain, currently and in the authors' view for the forseeable future, the second of these two courses is likely to be pursued. It will, however, not be fruitfully pursued unless teachers become more competent in assessment. Only in this way can the use of the evidence of assessment be extended from grading and selection to other major functions such as course evaluation and individual student diagnosis and guidance. Assessment will then become an integral part of the teaching/learning process instead of something alien to it.

The prime purpose of this book is, therefore, to try and provide teachers with the basic equipment to undertake assessment whether they wish to work within or outside an external examining system. Basic equipment is, however, of little use unless the environment within which it is to be used is a sympathetic one. Unless teachers believe that assessment is an essential part of their professional work they will not be willing to devote the time to it that its importance deserves. Nor will they be successful in persuading others, heads and local authorities for example, to provide them with the time, money and training facilities that professionally constructed assessment requires. This introduction is no place to discuss training provision but the point needs making that the form and level taken by training in assessment and its uses and the kind of support services needed to sustain the practical applications that ought to result from such training are of crucial importance.

The book starts by considering in the opening chapter the issues involved in defining objectives. This is followed by three chapters upon techniques. The first two are concerned with the methods of assessment currently in use and with the problems associated with their development. Examples are provided wherever possible and an indication given of the purpose(s) for which each method is most likely to be appropriate. The third describes, again with illustrations, simple ways of extracting as much information as possible from the results of assessment in order to use it to maximum advantage. The conclusion will outline ways in which the teacher in the classroom can use assessment. It thus seeks to reinforce explicitly points which the previous chapters have made implicitly. As this book is intended for the secondary teacher for whose pupils external examinations and professional entry qualifications will continue to remain facts of life, its main emphasis is upon the assessment of cognitive attainment although some consideration is given to practical skills and affective behaviours. It is hoped also that by looking at principles as well as practice it will encourage teachers to experiment with new approaches when assessing their own courses of study. A reading list related to each chapter is provided at the end of the book.

Chapter one

Objectives and assessment

Introduction

In the introduction it was suggested that the major purposes to which the results of assessment could be put were Diagnosis, Evaluation, Guidance, Grading, Prediction and Selection. The results of external examinations have been used almost exclusively for Grading and Selection and inevitably there has been a neglect of Diagnosis, Guidance and Evaluation although considerable informal use of assessment for these purposes has been made by teachers in the classroom. The evidence provided by assessment necessitates comparison but it is comparison that can take two basic forms. Performance can either be measured against the performance of a group, for example a nation, a school, an age group or a class or it may be measured against a fixed standard of mastery. Assessment which does the former is called norm referenced, assessment which does the latter is called criterion referenced. Most of our attainment assessment in the past has been norm referenced. Criterion referenced testing or mastery testing, to use another name for it, has, however, been used extensively in trade testing or for training purposes in, for example, the armed services. It is equally relevant to classroom practice. If, for example, one is developing programmed instructional materials, the routes to be used are determined by assessment of students' mastery or lack of mastery as shown in their answers to certain questions. Criterion referenced testing can also be combined with norm referenced testing to provide a series of course work hurdles which have to be mastered before a terminal test can be taken. In a course on educational measurement at MacQuarie University in Sydney, Australia, for example, all students have to take a series of tests which are related to sections of the course. An 80 per cent level of mastery is required and the test can be taken at any time chosen by the student within the course period up to a maximum of three times. For this purpose three forms of the test, equivalent in their demands, are used. In such a situation the students in addition to obtaining a result which will count towards their final degree obtain an immediate feedback upon their strengths and weaknesses in regard to the section being studied. This information is also available to the course instructors and can be used by them to review the course material and methods of instruction, and to identify and remedy individual student weaknesses. In such a situation assessment and learning are an integrated activity. Many opportunities exist for similar programmes in the classroom. The dependent elements of the process are illustrated simply in Furst's paradigm (1958) (see Figure 1).

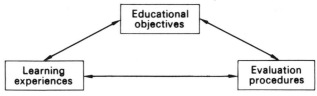

FIGURE 1

While the construction of criterion referenced tests poses problems which are different from those posed by normative tests (for example the necessity to secure discrimination between individuals in the former is less significant), the basic components of assessment remain the same, namely:

1 The objectives to be assessed;
2 The content within which these objectives are embedded;
3 The techniques used in making the assessment;
4 The weighting attached to each part of the assessment.

This chapter will be concerned primarily with the first two and the last of these four components while the next two chapters will be concerned with the techniques of assessment.

Defining objectives

If you were to look at the current syllabuses of any external examining board, whether it be a General Certificate of Education Board, a Certificate of Secondary Education Board, the Royal Society of Arts, the College of Preceptors or City and Guilds and compare them with the equivalent publications of say nine years earlier, you would notice a number of differences, not least the increasing range of subjects listed. Two differences are, however, particularly relevant to this chapter and these concern the presentation of the syllabuses themselves. In the earlier editions the syllabuses consist entirely of descriptions of content. Basically these descriptions constitute a contract between the examiner and the candidate, laying down those areas of study which the examiner is entitled to explore; at the same time they restrict the examiner to those areas which have been so laid down. Such a syllabus could be detailed or it could be limited, sometimes as limited as 'British History 1760–1920. The questions asked will be mainly upon political history but some knowledge of foreign affairs and economic and social topics will also be expected.' The teacher faced with this situation inevitably turns to past examination papers for amplification with all the undesirable possibilities that this raises. Clearly such syllabuses are examining and not teaching syllabuses. In the later editions, however, in some subjects and with some examining boards, notably the Joint Matriculation Board, alongside the content there will be found a statement of objectives which embodies a list of the skills or abilities which the examination proposes to test. An example of such a syllabus is as follows:

Physical Science (Ordinary) Joint Matriculation Board

The abilities to be tested

The following statement is intended to provide a general indication of the abilities which the examination will be designed to test in conjunction with the subject matter listed in the syllabus.

(a) *Knowledge*
- (i) Knowledge of appropriate scientific terminology
- (ii) Knowledge of the main facts that have been established about the subject
- (iii) Knowledge of the generalisations that have been made and the principles that have been established

(b) *Comprehension*
- (i) The ability to understand and interpret information presented in verbal, mathematical or graphical form and to translate such information from one form to another
- (ii) The ability to explain familiar phenomena in terms of the appropriate laws and principles which have been established

(c) *Application and Evaluation*
- (i) The ability to apply knowledge of facts, principles and laws to problems and to solve such problems in a verbal, mathematical or graphical manner
- (ii) The ability to construct explanations and hypotheses from given information

Three further sections then follow entitled: Weighting of the abilities; The form of the examination; Subject matter to be tested in the examination.

Syllabuses presented in this way are making a conscious effort to free teachers from a requirement to concentrate upon closely defined areas of contact and are thus encouraging them to teach their own courses in the ways they think most appropriate. Assessment can thus flow naturally from what is

4

taught. It needs nevertheless to be borne in mind that what is assessed, however extensive the techniques used to assess it, can only be a selection of what is taught. It is thus vital to ensure that this selection replicates the outcomes of any course as closely as possible. Ideally assessment ought to be a miniature and not an impression. It would, however, be unwise to assume that teachers automatically enjoy greater freedom in teaching courses based upon statements of objectives which lay down lists of abilities or skills. The very vagueness of the old style syllabus had advantages, particularly with pupils who were above average in ability.

Why these changes? Are they relevant to teachers in relation to their own courses? What are the supposed virtues of defining objectives? The short answer to this last question is that if people do not know where they are going or what they are doing, they will be unable to find out whether they have arrived or what they have achieved. In education, as in any other field of activity, people can learn a great deal from their mistakes. In order to do this, however, it is first of all necessary to identify the mistakes or the unsatisfactory features, whether they be in curriculum design, teaching methods or pupil performance and then correct or improve them. This means that evaluation must take place and therefore comparisons must be made. At some stage in every educational activity someone has to stand back and ask questions such as 'What are we doing?' 'How successful or unsuccessful are we being?' 'In what ways could we do better?' This can only be done if two things have happened:

1 That statements of what it is proposed should happen and of the objectives which it is hoped to achieve are in existence;
2 That these same statements have been set out, preferably in writing, so that others can read and discuss them.

It is not sufficient for the purposes of evaluation for individuals to say that they know what they are doing. They must be willing and in a position to ensure that others know as well.

Objectives and assessment

The last paragraph constitutes a typical justification for 'defining objectives'. Yet these arguments, apparently logical and full of commonsense, make singularly little appeal to many teachers. Before looking at the reasons for this and in so doing looking at the arguments against defining objectives, it is worth pausing and trying to clarify the terminology used, for in this lies part of the problem. In talking about defining objectives a large number of words or terms are used all too often as if they were interchangeable, the most common examples being 'aims', 'objectives' and 'behavioural objectives'. This can only cause confusion and unless people appreciate what others mean when they use particular words they can hardly be expected to think more clearly about the issues involved. It is not suggested that the definitions given here are better than others that could be provided but they may help. Most people when asked to justify a course of action or to solve a problem approach the matter initially in general rather than in specific terms and their first thoughts are, therefore, put forward in a rather general way. They then go on to work out in detail appropriate reasons or strategies. So it is with teachers in the classroom. When asked to justify their reasons for teaching a particular subject or setting a particular question or test, their initial responses tend to be given in general terms. It seems reasonable to call these general initial responses statements of aims. If then the question is asked how are these aims to be translated into course construction, teaching materials or patterns of assessment, then the responses, if they are to be worth anything, must become more concrete and specific. It seems equally reasonable to call these more concrete responses statements of objectives. Objectives thus apply to both teaching and assessment. The great problem in the past has been that the external examination has limited the range of teaching objectives. The possibility of extending this range will not, however, occur if teachers are unwilling to be systematic about what they are doing. The terminology as defined here is thus related to degrees of specificity (not a happy word but one for which no ready alternative comes to mind) and the most specific of the three terms referred to above is the behavioural objective to which we will return shortly.

Most discussions by teachers on the subject of defining objectives (and it is not always easy even to initiate such discussion) will contain remarks such as 'My subject is different (unique)', 'I know exactly what I am doing by instinct', or 'Most of the best results in my courses occur by chance and not as a result of advance planning', or 'Defining objectives means defining only what can be most easily assessed; everything really important is thus left out.' At some stage in the conversation the name of Bloom will be mentioned and is sure to provoke a mixed response, some grimacing while others smile with the fixed smile of the convert. These remarks, which it needs stressing, are not made lightly, reveal the disadvantages of defining objectives. The first of these concerns the degree of precision with which objectives can or ought to be stated. Here, as so often happens, ideas that were originally intended as aids to definition have proved counter-productive and aroused opposition. In the late 1950s and early 1960s a group of university examiners at Chicago led by Benjamin Bloom were seriously concerned about the lack of precision of their assessment and the unsystematic way in which questions were asked in examinations. As a guide they developed the first and still the best known classification of educational objectives. Bloom called these classifications 'taxonomies' (this is a word borrowed from the biological sciences which means an hierarchical and hence orderly classification). The Bloom taxonomies are divided into three areas or domains as he called them: I Cognitive, II Affective and III Psychomotor. The first two were published in 1956 and 1964 respectively while the third is not yet complete although other classifications in this area exist.

The cognitive domain with which most, although not all, classroom and external achievement testing is concerned deals with objectives having to do with knowing, thinking and problem-solving. The affective domain is concerned with objectives having to do with such things as attitudes, values, interests and reactions while the psychomotor domain is concerned with practical and manual skills. The structure of the Bloom taxonomies (and henceforward these remarks will be related to the cognitive domain only), with their emphasis upon outcomes of learning, lends itself very readily to the development of highly specific behavioural or performance objectives. Bloom's are, of course, not the only classifications of educational objectives: Gagné, for example, has an hierarchical one based upon types of learning and not outcomes. Gerlach and Sullivan base their system upon overt learner behaviours while Ebel bases his upon categories of examination questions. Despite their differences they all, however, emphasise a high degree of precision in their specification and are all, in consequence, artificial and rather too detailed for everyday use. Even those teachers who are willing (and they are slowly increasing in numbers), to adapt general classifications of objectives to their own subjects, to their own pupils and to their own schools, part company with the extreme advocates of behavioural objectives upon this issue of artificiality. For such advocates the statement of an objective has to have three basic characteristics. It must state:

1 An action performed by the student;
2 The conditions under which the performance is to occur;
3 The minimum level of acceptable performance.

The following would not be an acceptable specification for a behavioural objective: 'To demonstrate his ability to interpret a plan for a model, the student must be able to make the item depicted on the plan which will be given to him at the time of the examination. The student will be allowed to use all the tools in the workshop.'

This, on the other hand, would be acceptable: 'Given a human skeleton, the student must be able to identify correctly, by labelling, at least 40 of the following bones.' (A list of bones would then follow.)

The difference is that in the first example the criterion of acceptable performance is not stated while it is contained in the second.

Even allowing for the fact that more educationally significant examples could have been chosen it is obvious why this
kind of precision disturbs, to put it no more strongly, many
teachers. They consider, for example, that many aspects of the
teaching situation do not lend themselves to objective specification or to easy evaluation. They would also contend that
many of the more valuable outcomes of good teaching emerge
spontaneously and not as a result of pre-planning and
pre-specification. Moreover, the association of detailed specifications of objectives with evaluation and assessment
encourages the notion that it is the tail that is wagging the dog,
and that ease of assessment is what determines course content.
All this has led many teachers to reject out of hand the need
for precision at all, a need which in any case will vary greatly
from subject to subject. Because they feel that an attempt is
being made to provide definitive answers through the use of
artificial structures, they fail to take advantage of the stimulus
that exercises in being precise can provide for those who are
willing to go through with them. Flexibility is not a function
of the inexperienced and most people cannot afford the
luxury of being imprecise until they have tried to be precise.
The behavioural objective, moreover, has certain advantages
particularly in its emphasis upon the student rather than upon
the teacher. How often is assessment in the classroom
conducted with the teacher rather than the student in mind?
How often is it designed to show what students cannot do
rather than what they can achieve?

The wheel in education seems always to turn full circle and
so it is in relation to defining objectives. The need to define
objectives has been enthusiastically and uncritically accepted
by some and equally enthusiastically and uncritically rejected
by others. What is wanted is neither total acceptance nor total
rejection but a search for middle ground. Hogben in an article
in the May 1973 edition of the *Journal of Curriculum Studies*
offers some pertinent guidelines for such a middle ground.
Basically he is arguing not for acceptance or rejection of
classification systems such as those put forward by Bloom but
a search for more flexible systems which will embrace pupil

diversity in order to utilise the advantages that can result from greater definition and precision and minimise the disadvantages. He offers five suggestions to this end:

1 Course objectives should be stated by all means but it is not necessary that they are all stated in highly specific behavioural terms;
2 We should not be afraid to state long-term objectives;
3 We should be continually on the alert for unexpected or unintended outcomes;
4 In translating broad curricular goals into more specific language we should make sure that the sum of the objectives faithfully reflects the full intention of the original goals which gave them birth;
5 We should not allow measurement considerations alone to dictate the formulation of objectives and teaching strategies.

If, in the light of these general points, teachers were to consider their own courses in the context of subject, school and ability of pupils then they would be likely to consider the advantages and disadvantages of defining objectives in more rational and less emotive terms than has usually been the case in the past. It is certainly very easy to use objectives as standards of measurement instead of criteria for judgment. Different subjects undoubtedly do influence the degree of precision with which one can define. One has only, for example, to contrast Art and Physics. Not all worthwhile objectives are related to cognitive and practical skills which can be readily assessed. Published lists of objectives, even when adapted for subject use (see for example Coltham and Fines, 1971 or Wood, 1968) can be too mechanistic and too complex for practical use as they stand and need adaptation. But having said all this, precisely defined objectives have powerful advantages particularly when one is concerned with course evaluation or pupil assessment. They provide clear cut goals towards which pupils and teachers can jointly strive. Their influence in particular upon public examinations has been highly beneficial up to the present time.

It would be unwise, however, to assume that teachers' unwillingness to define objectives is solely related to dislike of the rigidity and limitations that can result from over-precision, powerful factor though this undoubtedly is. Two other issues are of significance and should be considered before leaving the whole question of defining objectives. These are as follows:

1 Ability versus knowledge in the assessment of educational achievement;
2 The relationship between precision and the purposes of assessment.

One of the features of defining objectives and of classification systems such as the Bloom taxonomies has been the diminished emphasis placed upon knowledge and the increased emphasis placed upon abilities and skills. The curriculum projects of the 1960s both in the USA and in Great Britain particularly in Science and Mathematics gave great weight to problem-solving and enquiry skills. These skills were strongly emphasised in the tests designed to evaluate the success of the projects and their associated materials or to assess pupil achievement during or following courses based upon them.

This influence showed itself, for example, in the JMB Physical Science Syllabus described earlier and would be reflected in the kind of questions set in the examinations based upon it. The great advantages of questions designed to test skills, according to their protagonists, is that they present those taking them with the information required to answer them rather than asking for it to be recalled. Obviously not all the relevant information can be presented through the questions but the emphasis is upon interpreting and using material rather than upon knowing and remembering it.

Those constructing tests and questions of this kind, however, soon run into practical difficulties. The need to present material tends to make the questions unnecessarily wordy and hence places a premium upon reading comprehension. More significantly the skills themselves prove far from easy to isolate particularly where detailed sub-divisions are involved and in consequence it is not easy to state with confidence that they have been tested. Such difficulties can be overcome by question-setting techniques as will be illustrated in the next chapter, and by introducing a sensible degree of generality into the description of what is to be tested. A good illustration of this is provided by the description in the JMB syllabus under Comprehension and Analysis which is in marked contrast to the detail provided under these same headings in the Bloom taxonomy.

Practical difficulties such as these have also thrown up some rather more fundamental issues for assessment. First of all, the terms 'knowledge' and 'ability', as Ebel points out, do not obviously refer to different aspects of human development and achievement, as some of those who denigrate the testing of knowledge and advocate instead the testing of abilities and skills would have us believe. The two indeed of necessity go hand in hand to a considerable extent. Those who have the greatest abilities in some field of activity always tend to be the most knowledgeable about it. To anyone, therefore, who is seeking to develop abilities, knowledge is an essential tool. Those who criticise teaching and assessment for their over-emphasis upon knowledge (and this has been a particularly long standing criticism of external examinations) have tended to define knowledge upon very narrow lines, and have implied that it is nothing more than rote retention and repetition, under instruction, of bits and pieces of disconnected information. Knowledge is much wider and more significant than that. It includes anything that a person has consciously expressed and remembered. Moreover, command of knowledge is not simply command of abstract concepts, it necessitates as well the ability to use and apply such concepts.

Even more important is the question of whether general abilities of the kind upon which the Bloom taxonomies are based exist at all in reality. Is there, as Ebel asks, any generality to the ability to choose means which serve a particular end? Is there an ability to recall major themes about particular cultures? If there is, how does it differ from the ability to recall the author of a particular book or the name that goes with a particular face? Is not an individual's ability to choose, to predict, to recall in a particular situation, almost entirely dependent upon his knowledge of that particular situation and almost totally independent of any general ability to choose, to predict or to recall? Cognitive abilities are quite specific to the area of knowledge in which they were developed. They transfer from one area of knowledge to another only to the extent that elements of knowledge in the two areas are similar or even identical.

It is arguments such as these that have caused thoughtful teachers to query the need for classifying educational objectives and hence to doubt the value of using such classifications as a basis upon which to devise frameworks for constructing assessment. They would advocate instead assessment which tested pupils' command of useful knowledge within the context of what had been taught. This is not of itself an argument against the careful planning of assessment but it is one which does not look receptively upon 'skills-based' testing or upon a behavioural approach to the defining of objectives.

Teacher reaction to defining objectives, in this country at least, is also as much bound up with the purposes of assessment as it is with the precision with which objectives ought or ought not to be stated. In our external examination system there has always been a dichotomy between the purpose(s) for which examinations were designed and the uses to which their results have subsequently been put. GCE and CSE examinations, for example, are designed to measure largely subject-based attainment at a particular point in time usually at the end of specific courses of study. Their results are, however, used as has already been indicated, both within schools and by outside users of all kinds, to select, grade, guide, diagnose, predict and evaluate, particularly to select and to grade. Moreover, our system of describing results by means of global grades (either numerical or lettered) makes it far easier for the user to add together results which are quite incompatible and call them something else. The fact also that our public examinations are essentially norm referenced rather than criterion referenced, adds to the potential unfairness of unsystematic and inappropriate usage.

Not surprisingly all this can easily create tensions for which teachers tend to blame the external examination system. In such circumstances examinations which are not carefully constructed upon specified objectives can be more readily, and ironically more fairly, used for a multiplicity of purposes than ones which are specified in more detail and with greater care.

The topic of defining objectives has been dealt with at considerable length in this opening chapter, not only because of its intrinsic importance in relation to assessment but because of its effect upon teacher attitudes to assessment in general. This, as was pointed out in the introduction, is fundamental not only to any lasting reform of our present examining system but also to the effective use of assessment by teachers in the classroom. As this chapter has tried to show, the teacher is beset by a number of important but contradictory arguments for and against defining objectives and indeed by a number of different definitions of 'defining objectives'. These arguments will, moreover, affect teachers differently according to the subject they teach and in relation to their views upon curriculum development, teaching methods and teaching materials. It is not surprising that under the circumstances teachers either take extreme standpoints for or against, or keep their heads down and try to carry on as normal.

The message of this chapter is basically that a continuation of this situation, while natural enough in the circumstances, will not solve any of the problems in the long run. If assessment is to meet the criterion of fitness for purpose, a criterion which is surely one which all concerned would be willing to endorse, then both thought and action needs to be taken about the purposes, planning and methods of assessment. The external examining agencies who are increasingly giving thought to planning and methods face considerable problems arising from the wide ranging nature of their target population. This, however hard they try, isolates them from individual schools and in catering for the mass on a largely external basis they cannot cater for the individual. It is for this reason that the most productive trend in modern external examining is, in the current jargon, the mixed Mode 1/Mode 3 or in more general terms a mixture of school and board assessment. Here the interaction between board and school in theory, and increasingly in practice, can range the whole way along the spectrum from totally board-based to totally school-based instead of remaining anchored firmly at one end or the other. Such a system requires that the areas within which school and board are to operate be clearly demarcated. If this is not done then some ground is likely to be covered twice while other ground will not be covered at all, thus making board moderation of the school work extremely difficult. This once again suggests that a more precisely defined pattern of assessment is necessary and returns us once more to our starting point of the four components of assessment, all of which must be in balance for the particular examining board/school/subject inter-action which is being considered. If this is more expensive in both time and money then it will be well worth while, in terms of its impact upon the quality of both teaching and assessment.

This chapter has concentrated so far upon objectives, the first of the four components of assessment outlined at its beginning. Substantial reference has also been made to the second component, content. Just as fitness for purpose is the key criterion in the determination of objectives so too is it all important in the choice of course content. The extent to which content is spelt out will vary as was suggested earlier according to whether it is presented for teaching or assessment purposes. Here in an external examining situation the interaction between examining board and school has important implications. The closer the interaction the more confident the teachers will be that what they are doing is what will be assessed and hence the less will be the need to spell out content in detail. The looser the instructions the less will be the confidence and the greater the need for detail. As already indicated the third component, techniques of assessment, will be the subject of the next two chapters. The fourth component, weighting, will now be briefly touched upon.

Weighting

'Weighting' is not in a sense a component at all. All the other components provide bits and pieces of the assessment framework; weighting is a feature of the framework itself. Any plan of assessment ultimately requires decisions to be taken about the relative weighting of its elements or, in other words, decisions have to be made about the value to be placed upon this particular aspect or that particular skill. In assessment the assigning of weighting usually takes the form of allocating X or Y marks or X per cent or Y per cent to a particular section. This X or Y should reflect not only the relative importance of what is being done but also the time taken to do it. It is unfair to those being assessed to make them devote a large amount of time to something for which they only receive 5 per cent of the available marks. Here the technique that is chosen for the assessment may be particularly relevant. Decisions about weighting are essentially subjective ones but if they are to make sense they must take account of earlier decisions made about the objectives of the course, the course content and the techniques of assessment to be used. These in their turn will have been made with specific pupils and subjects in mind. Determining relative weighting and actually achieving it in practice are two different things and it must again be reiterated that any assessment, however comprehensive it may be, is an assessment of only a sample, often a very small one, of the whole course. In practice weighting is determined by two things. First, the selection of appropriate methods of assessment which will permit and ideally encourage pupils to demonstrate degrees of mastery over the range of whatever it has been decided is to be assessed; second, the use of the full range of allocated marks. If assessment in, say, English is divided into four parts, Paper I

(Comprehension), Paper II (Essays on selected topics), Course work and Oral, and marks of 40, 60, 60, 40 out of a total of 200 are allocated to these parts respectively, this means that Parts 1 and 4 are supposed to be equally weighted as are Parts 2 and 3. This equal weighting will not be achieved in practice, however, if the mark range used in Part 2 is 55 (say lowest mark awarded 5, highest mark awarded 60), while that used in Part 3 is 20 (say lowest mark awarded 25, highest mark awarded 45). In these circumstances Part 2 will become more important in its influence on the assessment as a whole than Part 3. The important point to bear in mind is that preparations, however careful, will come to naught if inappropriate techniques are employed and the full range of allocated marks is not used.

Summary

This chapter has discussed such a wide range of issues that the overall picture it has presented may not stand out very clearly. It will perhaps therefore help to draw things together if in conclusion an example of a very fully developed syllabus and assessment scheme is given. In the recently introduced Parent Craft syllabus of the Southern Regional Examinations Board the details are well articulated.

Parent Craft

Aims

The aims of this course of studies are as follows:

1 To prepare students of both sexes for aspects of family life.
2 To encourage them to be aware of and to be sympathetic to the responsibilities which come with marriage, the birth of children and the establishment of a family unit.

3 To realise the value of a happy, healthy and stable family background in the physical, mental and moral development of the individual.

Objectives

The course not only has these overall aims in mind, but the candidates are expected to achieve the following educational objectives which the elements of the course are designed to assess:

1 A knowledge of the anatomy and physiology of the human body in relation to:
    (a) the development of both partners through adolescence to adulthood,
    (b) the process of procreation, and
    (c) child development and growth.
2 A knowledge of and an ability to evaluate the importance of the rules of health.
3 A knowledge of the causes of accidents in the home, methods of prevention and the practical ability to deal with them.
4 Practical ability in craft-work to enable the child to produce equipment for the nursery, and also toys and garments.
5 A knowledge of the stages of a child's intellectual development and the modes of learning appropriate to each stage.
6 A knowledge of the psychological development of the child and the ability to select the appropriate solution for behavioural problems in the context of family life.
7 An understanding of the contribution which an inadequate family life can make towards social problems, e.g. drug-taking, delinquency.
8 A knowledge of the tensions created by the interaction of personalities within a family, their possible consequences and the contribution which the supportive services can make.
9 A knowledge of the decisions which might have to be

made leading up to marriage, in marriage and in family life, e.g. the choice of a partner, size of family, division of responsibilities, etc., and an ability to establish priorities in decision-making.

10 The ability to evaluate the moral and social issues basic to the existence of a family (e.g. the sanctity of life, population explosion, etc.)

Facilities

1 It is felt that this course will be best handled by an Integrated Studies team of staff in which Home Economics, Science and Humanities departments would play a major part or, alternatively, interrelated contributions from all three areas. In either case it is important that overall direction is given to ensure the balance of the course.

2 Attention is drawn to resources available to schools through local Health Departments and to the availability of qualified staff working in a number of associated areas, who are often prepared to help.

3 In order to give full scope to the practical objectives of the course, visits and work experience in clinics, nurseries, day nurseries, pre-school playgroups and local infant schools should be explored to the full.

4 It is suggested that an appropriate time allocation for this course would be 4 periods a week over 2 years, preferably blocked.

Content

The following is intended as a guide to achieving the objectives listed. The extent to which staff develop each section will depend on individual circumstances. Numbers listed at each section heading refer to the appropriate objectives. This should not be regarded as exclusive.

Section 1   *Preparation for marriage* (objectives 1(a); 9; 10)

01 Simple anatomy and physiology

Objectives and assessment

02 General health — VD, drugs, smoking, etc. — effects on health

03 The engagement — choosing a partner — hereditary diseases, etc.

04 Marriage — meaning, preparation, etc., the ceremony

Section 2   The family (objectives 1(b); (c); 2; 7; 8; 9; 10)

05 Contraception — various methods. Objections — disadvantages

06 Conception

07 Normal pregnancy — pre-natal health

08 Arrangements for delivery

09 Birth

10 Father's role during pregnancy and birth

Section 3   Caring for the child (objectives 1(c); 2; 3; 4)

11 Layette, equipment and the nursery

12 Safety measures

13 Hygiene of the child's environment

14 Personal hygiene of the child

15 Normal stages of physical development

16 Infant feeding, e.g. breast feeding; artificial feeding; weaning

17 Basic dietetic requirements

18 Minor accidents and first aid

19 Minor ailments

20 Symptoms and signs of common infectious diseases

21 Supportive services for the family

Section 4   The child growing up (objectives 3; 5; 6; 8)

22 The behaviour of the new born child

23 Norms of spontaneous development, e.g. sight; hearing; touch; sitting; walking

24 Individual differences in the stages of physical development of children

25 Emotional development of the child and how care and environment affect this by association with adults;

other children; dependence; independence; discipline
and self control; family relationships; common causes
of children's behavioural difficulties

Section 5   The child learning (objectives 5; 6)

26 Learning at home. The supreme importance of the
good mother; some common defects at home; the only
child; adult environment; erratic and harsh discipline;
the slum

27 The value of the nursery and nursery school

28 Simple guidance on the main training problems relating
to:

(a) Play: freedom to play and to let others play;
child's care of toys; use of educative apparatus; use
of organised play activities; physical; imaginative;
manipulative play; co-operative play

(b) Speech: importance of example; common
impediments

(c) Use of specific educative 'material' – sand, clay,
plasticine, dough, water, etc.

(d) Nursery rhymes: origin and significance; basic
requirements

(e) Music and basic movement: rhythm, percussion;
songs and games; organisation of a typical 'session'

(f) Make-believe: story telling; dramatics

(g) Books: stories and poetry; 'good' literature;
pleasing art

(h) Art: drawing and painting techniques; tearing,
cutting, pasting, mounting

(i) Conduct of meals and birthday parties, Hallowe'en
and Christmas parties. Tables; decorations; games
planning; picnics

29 The outdoors: the nature table; care of pets;
responsibility to animals

Assessment
Assessment of the objectives is to be by the following
methods:

Objectives and assessment

1 Written paper to be issued by the Board.
2 Oral to be conducted by a person other than staff teaching the course, by agreement with the local consortium, according to guidelines to be issued by the Board.
3 Practicals 3 practical tests for periodic assessment, issued by the Board to test (i) dietetics and (ii) the care of the young child.
4 Craft work craft work produced during the course to be assessed at local consortium moderation.
5 Folder to be the student's record of child development as seen in visits.
6 Observation unobtrusive assessment by observation of the candidate in the course of visits.
7 Discussion teacher assessment of the candidate in 'discussion' situation.

Note: For assessment (2), (6) and (7) profiles of assessment will be issued by the Board to schools.

The following grid links the methods of assessment to the objectives. It also gives the weightings for each of the objectives and for each of the methods of assessment:

| Objectives | Theory | | Discussion | Practice | | | Weighting of objective |
	Written paper	Oral		Practical and craft work	Folder	Assessment by observation	
1	7	3					10
2	5			10			15
3	5	5					10
4				10			10
5	2	2					13
6			5		6	3	11
7	2		6		4	2	8
8	4		4				8
9			7				7
10			8				8
Weighting of method of assessment	25	10	30	20	10	5	100
	35%		30%	35%			

As will be seen this syllabus covers the four components, objectives, content, techniques and weighting. Under the heading of facilities it also provides information which is intended to prevent an over restrictive interpretation of the objectives. Several other important features of this syllabus deserve mention:

1 The content is given as a guide to achieving the objectives;
2 The objectives covered in each section of the syllabus have been indicated;
3 The assumption is made that the course concerned is a two year one;
4 It is essentially an examination blueprint and not a teaching syllabus. A school envisaging the development of say a five year course in Parent Craft would need to elaborate its outline considerably, particularly in relation to the teaching strategies to be adopted, the materials to be used and the nature of the assessment to be adopted. Greater emphasis might for example be placed upon criterion referenced measures designed primarily to improve the course and help students rather than to grade them for certification purposes;
5 The detail under the heading 'Assessment' is very general in scope being concerned rather more with approaches than with specific methods. Indeed the use of a course folder makes this essential, for such an approach can involve oral, written and practical work within its ambit;
6 In the grid the weighting to be given to each of the objectives is not only indicated but is also related to the method of assessment to be used.

The Parent Craft syllabus, while elaborate, is essentially a practical working document and it will have failed in its purpose if those studying it do not consider it to be such. However, looking at other people's specifications, no matter how well prepared and appropriate they may seem to be, is no substitute for producing one's own. It is recommended therefore that readers, after they have completed this book, choose courses of their own and plan out an overall course and assessment blueprint, starting with the objectives and including content, techniques of assessment and weighting as appropriate. Merely attempting this will be of far more value than any written or verbal advice. The need to carry out in practical terms the points made in this book and in any other reading or discussion undertaken is absolutely essential if the exercise is not to remain theoretical and academic.

Chapter two

Techniques of assessment   I

Introduction

If we use the analogy of a completed building for an examination or assessment programme then the next two chapters are concerned with the building materials, namely the techniques that are available for use in assessment. There are, however, a number of general issues that require consideration at the outset which relate to the building itself. There are, first, the two key concepts of balance and structure and, second, the question of when to assess. This opening section will then be followed by a brief consideration of the techniques available for assessing cognitive attainment. This chapter will cover written assessment while Chapter 3 will be concerned with oral and practical assessment. A concluding section at the end of Chapter 3 will be devoted to the assessment of attitudes which, apart from their intrinsic importance in education, have in recent years become increasingly a feature of public examinations particularly in Science and the Humanities. There is no specific section devoted to the assessment of physical skills but the general principles discussed and much of the detail provided are as relevant here as they are to cognitive and attitudinal assessment.

Balance and structure

However well planned and comprehensive assessment programmes may be they cannot conceivably take account of all the available evidence and must therefore select. As has already been stressed it is particularly important that the chosen part be as representative of the whole as possible, if not the picture presented by the assessment will be a distorted one. This need to make the replication a faithful miniature applies not only to the selection of content and skills but also to the techniques of assessment proposed. All techniques benefit some and are disadvantageous to others; hence an appropriate balance needs always to be sought. Balance indeed is a key concept in the construction of assessment. The ideal assessment programme is one which secures an equilibrium in terms of its demands and in terms of the kinds of responses which it provokes. Such an equilibrium is not easy to secure. It requires not only knowledge of pupil and subject and the techniques available but also careful planning. The Parent Craft blueprint contained in Chapter 1 represents the kind of blueprint that public examining bodies ought to produce for all their syllabuses. Similar, if less elaborate, blueprints ought also to be produced by teachers both for the overall assessment of their own courses and for particular tests within those courses. As with the Parent Craft proposal such blueprints should contain details of the objectives to be covered, the content, the techniques of assessment to be used and their relative weighting. The preparation of such blueprints, as has already been emphasised, is not something which individual teachers can do satisfactorily on their own. It must involve collaboration with colleagues.

The second key concept in the construction of assessment is that of structure. The degree of 'structure' in the assessment determines the room for manoeuvre given to those responding to the task put before them. In the classroom teaching situation it is possible to approach any topic from two extreme standpoints. The first is to spell out through formal didactic teaching the important features of the topic concerned, if necessary dictating them in note form and then requiring the pupils to learn the detail by heart. The relative success or failure of this approach is easily assessed. The second is to tell the pupils nothing about the topic beyond its title and ask them to find out all they can about it. This is much less easily assessed because of the difficulty of deciding upon the relative worth of totally different responses. These two approaches represent the two extremes of structure. The first is highly structured in that the pupil's room for manoeuvre and independent thought is severely limited. The second on the other hand is very loosely structured and the pupil is in consequence left with almost limitless room for manoeuvre being only constrained by the nature of the topic itself. Most teaching however does not lie at these extremes, it rests instead somewhere between the two. The teacher introduces more or less structure into the situation according to the needs of the subject and the pupils, at times talking, at times listening, at times supplying material, at times withholding it. As it is with teaching so should it be with assessment. We have tended in the past to make use of assessment techniques which have demanded either an extremely closed or an extremely open response and have tended to neglect those which vary the nature of the response according to the needs of the situation.

When to assess

It is as important to determine when to assess as it is to determine how to assess. What for example are the relative merits of terminal, periodic and continuous assessment? These can be more readily determined if the meanings of the three terms are defined at the outset. Terminal assessment is much the easiest to define and, largely as a consequence, is much the most commonly used. It is a measure or a number of measures of attainment at the end of a course. Periodic assessment is usually intended to provide a similar measure of attainment but by means of a series of intermittent probes taken at intervals throughout a course. Currently continuous assessment is both popular and ill-defined. Because it means different things to different people it is regarded by many as the panacea for all the ills of terminal tests and set-piece examinations. What is less immediately obvious is that it must by its very nature involve the pupil's own teacher and hence can affect the pupil-teacher relationship. It would seem reasonable to regard it as the continuous updating of judgments about pupil performance in relation to specific criteria which will permit a cumulative judgment to be made upon these same criteria. At the same time continuous assessment demands and benefits from great flexibility in its operation. Rogers (in Macintosh, ed., 1974, Chapter 9) likens it to the progress of a missile. As the missile homes on to its target it rarely follows the path originally planned for it. Its course is constantly modified by feedback provided from its previous path. A similar process of modification resulting from feedback ought to take place in education and unless the assessment programme is sufficiently flexible it cannot provide useful feedback and hence cannot point to appropriate modifications.

If the definition of continuous assessment given in the previous paragraph is acceptable then it has important implications for assessment. First, the continuous updating of judgments upon students' work can only be undertaken realistically if teachers are willing to maintain careful and comprehensive records. The issue of the pupil-teacher relationship is therefore raised again. This hinges largely upon the competence of the teacher in assessment and upon the uses to which the results of the assessment are to be put. A second problem that can arise is that of additional pressure upon pupils. It is not always easy for teachers to resist an 'if it moves assess it' approach to continuously-assessed courses of study and this may result in much greater burdens being placed upon many pupils than would result from a terminal examination. A third and more fundamental problem arises from the fact that not all subjects lend themselves to the use of continuous assessment. There are within all school curricula both linear and cyclical subjects. A linear subject, of which Mathematics, Physics and Geography are examples, is composed of modules each one of which while independent of the others contributes naturally to the development of the subject as a whole. A student studying Physics can study light, heat and magnetism quite independently of one another. The body of knowledge is extended by the study of further related facets of the subject. A cyclical subject, on the other hand, of which English and languages in general are examples, is one in which the body of knowledge is indivisible and in consequence improvement in pupils' competence in the subject comes from the development of their ability to manipulate the basic tools. More sophisticated ways of using these tools may be acquired, but they cannot be divorced from the totality of the subject.

Continuous updating in respect of a linear subject would seem therefore impracticable. To use Physics as an example, it is difficult having undertaken the assessment of the first module studied, say, heat, then subsequently to update it in the light of work done on the second module, say, magnetism. In such circumstances one can only take the student's temperature as it were on a number of occasions throughout the course under different conditions and at the end of the day convert them into a global judgment as to whether or not the pupil showed any signs of becoming a physicist. In assessment terms this is no smooth flowing stream but rather a series of cataracts. It may be, of course, that while the content of the modules differs, the skills required remain the same. Even if this were the case it would still create difficulties for continuous assessment, since certain modules might be more appropriate for demonstrating certain skills than others. The skills would thus come into prominence in relation to both teaching and assessment at different stages of the course and hence could only be assessed at intervals.

In effect, therefore, much of what passes for continuous assessment is periodic or intermittent. This may appear to be a play upon words but it is significant for the relationship between assessment and teaching. Periodic assessment has to be very well planned if it is to be fully integrated with teaching. This requires the components of assessment referred to in Chapter 1 to be brought into play both in relation to the parts that go to make up the total pattern of assessment as well as to the whole itself. The significance of Hogben's suggestion in Chapter 1 that we do not lose sight of the whole because of our interest in the parts, becomes once again apparent. Such an approach, as already suggested, is much more suited to departmental or school activity than to the work of a single individual. Both input and output will be greatly increased if several teachers are involved.

The nature of assessment

Assessment is essentially an exercise in communication. Instructions or stimuli are given in a variety of forms to those being assessed. The responses to these instructions or stimuli are then evaluated, described or compared according to the purposes of the assessment. These instructions or stimuli can be provided orally or in writing or through the use of visual material such as pictures, photographs, diagrams, drawings and the like. These different methods can be used on their own or in combinations, for example a photograph accompanied by a number of written questions. They may require facts to be given by way of response, or arguments to be rehearsed. They may seek out opinions or attitudes or ask for solutions to problems. They may require the production of a physical object or the undertaking of a task. Writing a composition, making a speech, baking a cake, providing opinions upon the policies of the current government or upon a new detergent, taking a photograph, building a boat, playing Macbeth, running the hundred yards (either simply running it or running it in under eleven seconds), setting up equipment for a scientific experiment and then undertaking it, are all possible responses to instructions or stimuli which can be assessed either on their own or in relation to other similar responses. The responses can then be quantified and used in a variety of ways for a variety of purposes.

In teaching and in assessment, both in the classroom and in public examinations, the cognitive outcomes of education have been pre-eminent. This pre-eminence which indeed is reflected in the contents of this book may, however, be in marked contrast to the aims of education where the main emphasis is sometimes placed upon affective objectives and where in various ways the education of the whole person is frequently extolled. Rarely, if ever indeed, can a single human behaviour be said to consist solely of thinking or feeling or doing (the three main divisions of the outcomes of education). It will consist instead of elements of all three but always with a different mix or emphasis. If we are not to distort the aims of the curriculum developers then our assessment programmes ought to reflect these stated aims to a far greater extent than is usually the case at present. The techniques used for assessing affective behaviours and physical skills are on occasion different from those required for the assessment of cognitive skills and attainment. In the case of affective behaviours, moreover, the act of assessment itself is likely to arouse more emotions. The general principles of assessment none the less remain the same. The need, for example, to be as precise as possible in defining what one is trying to do and to prepare blueprints to implement one's proposals, is as relevant for the assessment of say persistence as it is for testing students' knowledge of the dates of the kings and queens of England.

Neither classroom assessment nor external examinations have in the past exploited the variety suggested earlier because they have limited the range of responses by the type of instructions they have issued and the stimuli they have supplied. Most assessment moreover tends to be terminal in character and thus fails to take advantage of the possibilities of planned assessment throughout a course. In particular there has been an over-emphasis upon written instructions. A convention moreover has developed that responses should be provided in the same medium as instructions, that is to say that an oral question should be answered orally and a written question in writing. There has also developed in public examinations at least, a further convention that different types of question should be separated from each other, e.g. that written questions should be contained in a different section of the examination from oral ones. This has even been carried a stage further and different types of written and oral questions

31

tend to be separated from each other in the same examination, for example objective items have a separate section of their own away from the essays. The justification for this has been that those taking the assessment ought not to be confused by a variety of different instructions for answering the questions and should instead be given a clear run at questions requiring one such set only. We ought, however, to ask ourselves whether this is a natural activity. Does such a separation occur in the classroom? Surely pupils if left to themselves, move freely from one type of response to another according to the type of situation and the naturalness of the medium for response.

Instructions, stimuli and responses can be divided into three broad categories, written, spoken and practical, and most books on assessment treat techniques and methods under general headings such as these. Provided it is appreciated that it is more usually the responses and not the methods used to stimulate them that are being described, then this division provides a convenient framework within which to look at the range of methods currently in use for the assessment of attainment at the secondary level and at some of the problems associated with their construction. Each of these three categories will therefore be considered in turn, aural being looked at under the spoken section and projects as a form of practical work. As already indicated there will be a brief concluding section on the assessment of affective behaviours.

The construction of any kind of assessment and its assembly into an overall test or programme is a skilled task. It requires

1 Knowledge of the subject matter proposed for assessment;
2 Appreciation of the abilities proposed for assessment;
3 Experience of the teaching situation in relation to the ability and age of the pupils being assessed and the subject being taught;
4 Collaboration with fellow practitioners.

These are not of course requirements that can be met merely

by reading a single textbook however comprehensive it may be. Such skills emerge from experience and are fostered by practice, wide reading and discussion. Such activities will, however, be time well spent since improved assessment will be reflected in improved teaching and learning. All that a book of this nature and length can hope to do is to make a series of practical suggestions for use as general guidelines. These suggestions must never be regarded as laws which cannot be broken; some indeed are mutually exclusive. When in doubt common sense and the criticism of experienced colleagues will provide the best guidelines. Although examples will be given these will necessarily be limited and readers should always relate the points made to their own subjects and to their own situations. There are, however, two basic commandments and although it would be untrue to say that upon these hang all the law and the prophets there is no doubt in the authors' minds that their adoption and rigorous application in conjunction with the more specific points made in the sections which follow, would eliminate many of the errors currently found in the construction of assessment. This would be particularly true of written questions which form a major part of most attainment assessment. These two are as follows:

1 Aim at absolute clarity in the presentation of the assessment;
2 Make sure that *all* the information provided for those being assessed is relevant.

Written assessment

In most books on assessment written assessment, which is concerned exclusively with question and response, is divided into three sections, usually called 'Objective or Short Answer Questions', 'Structured Questions' and 'Open-Ended or Essay Questions'. Here written questions will be considered initially as a whole in relation to the degree of structuring which they provide. This approach throws up sets of criteria against which the questions can be judged. In looking at written questions the term 'open' is used to describe questions which provide those answering them with considerable scope for manoeuvre, while the term 'closed' describes questions which provide very little scope for the answerer. The open/closed continuum does not, however, bear any relationship to hierarchies of skills of the kind put forward by Bloom and others. Moreover, the degree of openness or closedness ought not to be associated specifically either with the ease or difficulty of the question concerned or with the precision of its wording.

What then are the characteristics of a written question near the closed end of the spectrum? First of all it is likely to ask those responding to it to select material or information from a given set. The most extreme example of structuring is when the selection takes place from two given alternatives (the true/false objective item). Second, it is likely to ask respondents to read more than they write. Third, it is likely to be relatively easy to mark but relatively difficult to construct, and fourth, each question will cover a relatively limited area. It follows that if these characteristics for a closed question are accepted the characteristics of a question at the open end of the spectrum will be the reverse, in other words respondents will be asked to supply material or information of their own in order to answer the question; they will be required to do more writing than reading; the questions are likely to be difficult to mark but relatively easy to set and they will be relatively wide ranging in their demands. The significance of these points can readily be tested by taking questions at the extremities like '"Physics is Fun", Discuss' (open), and '"The author of *Oliver Twist* was Charles Dickens" YES/NO' (closed). The points suggested above will provide four sets of criteria against which to judge written questions and hence a framework upon which to hang them. These four sets of criteria, all of which relate to demands posed by the questions, are:

Selecting answers	↔	Supplying answers
Marking demands	↔	Setting demands
Amount of reading	↔	Amount of writing
Wide ranging in demands	↔	Limited in demands

Concealed within these criteria are the two very important concepts of Validity and Reliability.

Reliability is a relatively simple concept and may be defined as the consistency with which a set of test scores measures whatever it does measure. There are several factors which can cause unreliability but the one which is shown up particularly within the listed criteria is that occasioned by marking. The use therefore of questions which make considerable demands upon marking requires justification to offset a likely increase in unreliability. Validity is a more complex and a more important concept in assessment. It can be very tightly defined as the accuracy with which a test measures what it is intended to measure or as the degree to which it approaches infallibility in measuring what it purports to measure. This suggests that in order to determine validity one must compare the reality of what it does measure with some ideal conception of what it ought to measure. This, of course, leaves on one side the question of what the test should be measuring in the first place. Physical scientists, however, more accurate than most in their measurement, do not worry about that kind of validity. They tend to worry about how accurate and how useful are their measures rather than about the essentially unsolvable question of what they purport to measure. This view is echoed in another definition which states 'by validity we refer to the extent to which the measuring device used is useful for a given purpose'. A dictionary states that a test or anything else is valid if it is founded on truth or fact, capable of being justified, supported or defended, well grounded, sound. Definitions such as these broaden the concept of validity and permit a formulation which may be of more practical value in classroom assessment. The big difference between reliability and validity is that the latter is essentially a matter of degree. There is no such thing as an absolutely valid test. There are simply tests which are more or less valid.

In using criteria such as those suggested earlier one has to buy one advantage at the expense of another. If, for example, the marking demands are reduced then the setting demands are likely to be increased. If the writing demands are reduced then the reading demands are likely to increase. As always it is balance that is all important and one of the key determinants in striking the right balance is the achievement of validity.

In the past, public examinations have tended to over-use the essay question while teachers in their weekly or daily classroom quizzes have equally tended to over-use the short answer question. Both these types of question have the advantages and disadvantages already described which relate to their position at the open and closed ends of the continuum respectively. More recently there has been a move towards the setting of questions which are to be found in the middle of the continuum. These are frequently referred to as structured questions. Their principal advantage is that they can replicate the kind of structuring that teachers use in the classroom. They are thus intended to achieve a closer relationship between teaching, learning and assessing. Typically such questions ask those responding to them to study information which is provided for them. Sometimes this information is familiar, sometimes unfamiliar. They are then required to use this information in answering a series of questions (usually some four to eight in number) which progressively test their understanding. Most structured questions are thus not single questions but rather sets of questions based upon common material. Material and questions can and ought to be tailored more closely to the needs of both courses and pupils than is possible when using more open or more closed questions. This important advantage is however not easily bought. Structured questions are probably the most difficult of all written questions to set whilst their marking cannot be completely objective. An example of a set of structured questions will be given later in this chapter.

Pretesting

Another recent feature of the construction of examinations which make use of written questions is pretesting. Pretesting simply means trying out questions in advance upon those who will subsequently be taking the examination or upon a group as similar as possible in composition to them (in age, sex, type of school, ability range, for example). The information gained is then put to use in the construction of the actual examination. Pretesting of an informal kind has always been carried out by those who set questions for their own use or for public examinations. Questions are tried out upon pupils as a part of normal classroom activity and some feel at least about their likely difficulty and the clarity or otherwise of their wording is obtained. It was not until the introduction of objective testing in this country on a sizeable scale in the late 1960s that formal pretesting and systematic analysis became a normal part of test construction for examinations which involved their use.

Apart from information about question ease or difficulty and their relative ability to discriminate between pupils, pretesting enables deficiencies in the wording of questions to be detected and provides detail about the possible timing of the examination and/or its component parts. The value of this information has resulted in work being undertaken upon the analysis of more open questions (Nuttall and Willmott, 1972) and we can expect to see a considerable extension of pretesting in the future. For most teachers in the classroom, however, the procedures adopted by public examining bodies for pretesting and analysis are out of the question. Much the same information can however be obtained less elaborately after the questions have actually been answered in the examination itself (post testing). It is perfectly possible moreover preferably as a collaborative exercise, for teachers to record this information in permanent form upon cards and to develop a store or bank of proven questions for future use. This will be discussed in Chapter 4.

The construction of written questions

Some key points in the construction of written questions will now be considered, using for convenience the three headings, 'Objective Items', 'Structured Questions' and 'Open-ended Questions' under which to do it. An objective item (item is the term more commonly used than question) as defined here is one which is asked in such a way that for it there is only one predetermined correct answer. This definition rules out any question which requires an answer to be supplied however short; decisions are needed in the marking of such questions even if only to determine acceptable degrees of incorrect spelling. It needs emphasising at this point that the only thing that is objective about an objective item or test is its marking, everything else about it involves the taking of subjective decisions, for example what to include and what to exclude in the options. Short answer questions although not considered as a separate heading, will be covered under 'structured questions', many of whose parts require short answers and in the general points made upon question setting.

The points made under 'objective items' will be concerned solely with the multiple choice item. This particular objective item format which will be described in detail is by far the most flexible of all those in current use and anyone wishing to construct objective items would be wise to concentrate on this format before trying other item types such as true/false, multiple completion and assertion/reason, examples of which can be found in the suggestions for further reading.

Objective items – multiple choice

A multiple choice item consists of a stem in the form of a question or incomplete statement, e.g. 'Which of the following statements best describes Palmerston's foreign policy?' or 'In the early nineteenth century the Eastern question was created mainly by the ———' followed by four or five possible answers or completions, one of which is right (the key) and the others of which are wrong (the distractors). Rightness or wrongness is of course strictly related to the question or completion to which the answers refer. The key and the distractors together are known as the options as the following example shows:

Stem		What was meant in the nineteenth century by 'payment by results'?
Distractor	A	Higher wages for workers on piece-work
Key	B	Government grants for efficient schools
Distractor	C	Higher dividends at Co-operative stores for the best customers
Distractor	D	Tax allowances for large families
Distractor	E	Free medical treatment for those injured as a result of industrial accidents

The setting of multiple choice items presents three particular problems which are not significant in the setting of other types of written questions, namely the need to ensure that

1 The distractors are plausible;
2 All the options are parallel;
3 Clues are not given to the respondent.

1 Normally when setting questions the primary concern is with the questions and not with the answers. With a multiple choice item both the correct answer or key and the distractors are of equal importance. This greatly increases the item writer's problems but it also greatly increases the value of such items in the classroom situation. The reasons both for the choice of the key and for the rejection of the distractors can provide much valuable information to teachers about the strengths and weaknesses of their pupils and of their teaching methods. If a distractor is so implausible that even the least able can eliminate it as a possible correct answer then it will have contributed nothing of use to the item. The best sources of plausible distractors are the common misconceptions of one's own pupils and these can easily be obtained by rephrasing multiple choice items in a short answer form and noting the answers given. There is no magic in having five rather than four options although five increases the mathematical odds against the guesser. The important point is to

ensure that all the chosen options are plausible and with some subjects, for example Mathematics and Science, it may be easier to find five than with others.

2   In many subjects the traditional examination has consisted of some twelve essay questions from which the pupils had to select perhaps up to five to answer in some 2½ hours. These questions are usually wide ranging in their scope, and hope for a similar wide range in the answers obtained. In consequence it is easy to forget that a test consisting of multiple choice items can contain as many as forty or fifty to be answered at a rate of about one a minute. Each individual item should therefore be concerned with one specific point and not a number of unrelated factors. The way to ensure that this is done is to make certain that the stem poses the problem clearly. For the person who is starting to write items this is often more easily done if the stem takes the form of a question rather than one requiring a completion. For example if the stem reads 'The Battle of Hastings took place in' it provides no guidance at all for the pupil who cannot know what kind of answer is required (see the first of the two commandments). It is also an open invitation to the item writer to use non-parallel options as for example

A	thick fog	—	weather
B	Kent	—	county
C	1066	—	year
D	the eleventh century	—	century

These may seem rather ridiculous but it is all too easy to make this mistake. If the stem is set out in the form of a crisp question, i.e. 'In what year did the Battle of Hastings take place?' not only is the requirement of the item clear to the pupil but there is little risk of the item writer using non-parallel options.

3   A poor item can give clues to the intended correct answer in a wide variety of ways for example

1 by the use of stereotyped wording which a pupil may have learnt by heart (taking the wording of an option

direct from a text book is a good example of this);
2 by making the correct option always the longest;
3 by placing the correct option in some definite sequence within a test, e.g. ABCD, ABCD or AAAB, CCCD;
4 by using options which are grammatically inconsistent with the stem (singular/plural is the most common).

Even the most experienced item writer can fall into traps such as these. The preparation of detailed blueprints and the use of editorial criticism are therefore essential. The latter in a school situation can be provided by colleagues, with whom co-operation should take place on a reciprocal or team basis. As with writing, editing items is a skilled task and the requirements are very much the same with the important proviso that while the writer's work is primarily creative the editor's task is that of criticism, albeit constructive criticism.

The most frequently made criticism of objective items is that the correct answer can be guessed. (What incidentally do we mean by guessing? Blind chance or taking advantage of part knowledge and understanding?) A great deal has been written about this issue from both a mathematical and a non-mathematical standpoint and the interested reader should refer to, for example, Ebel, 1972 and Macintosh and Morrison, 1969. The authors believe, however, that the crucial factor lies in the items themselves and it should be remembered that an objective test will normally contain at least forty items. They would argue that if all these were well constructed, of appropriate difficulty for the group taking them and tested something worthwhile, then those answering them would be unlikely to resort to wild and uninformed guessing. Concern for construction is thus more important than concern about guessing.

Structured questions

Some features of the structured question have already been referred to. The effect of these upon the setting of such

Techniques of assessment I

questions can best be illustrated by looking at two examples, both of which are intended for pupils aged 15–16. The first of these is taken from Physics and illustrates a typical set of questions based upon common material, in this case a diagram. Following the set is the suggested mark scheme and a note of the skills being tested by each question.

This group of questions is based on an investigation into the effect of an electric current on a concentrated solution of lead II chloride in water, at a temperature between 90°C and 95°C, using the apparatus shown in the figure.

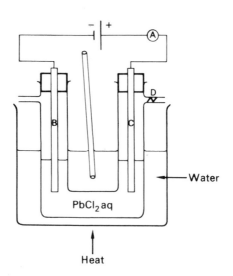

1 What *general* name is given to the two pieces of apparatus B and C?

....

2 What *particular* name would be given to the piece of apparatus C?

....

3 Name a suitable material of which *both* B and C could be made.

....

4 What purpose is served by the moist litmus paper at D?

....

5 Suggest a reason for heating the U-tube by surrounding it with hot water rather than heating it directly by a bunsen.

....

....

6 What would you expect to be formed on B?

....

7 When the temperature of the solution was allowed to fall, the current flowing through A decreased. Suggest *two* possible reasons for this.

....

....

....

8 This electrolysis resembles a change which takes place when a piece of zinc is placed into a solution of lead II

chloride. State and explain *one* similarity.

....

....

....

Marking scheme

1. Electrodes   — 1 mark
2. Anode   — 1 mark
3. Carbon, but allow any other inert electrode material

      — 1 mark
4. To test for chlorine   — 1 mark
5. Two marks for a valid reason, e.g. to get easier control or to get uniform heating; allow one mark for reasons which are not of prime importance but have some relevance   max. — 2 marks
6. Lead   — 1 mark
7. Fall in concentration of ions or lowering of solubility of lead chloride   — 1 mark
   Fall in mobility of ions   — 1 mark
8. One mark for a reasonable similarity; the most likely one being the formation of lead
   Two marks for a valid explanation e.g. both zinc and a cathode provide electrons for the change: max. — 3 marks

$$Pb^{2+}(aq) + 2e^- \rightarrow Pb(s)$$

One mark for partly complete explanation

(It is suggested that the questions in this set test the following:

1. Knowledge
2. Knowledge
3. Comprehension
4. Comprehension
5. Application
6. Comprehension
7. Application
8. Application)

As with the multiple choice item, the setting of structured questions throws up certain problems which are not present in the construction of other types of written questions. With the structured question these are:

1 the interaction between material and questions, and
2 the sequencing of the questions.

The latter applies only when a set of questions is involved. Teaching should require pupils to work on information rather than simply to recall it. A structured question set will therefore supply the pupil at the outset with information; this may be added to or modified after the first few questions. The information must have some worth in itself but it must also be capable of being exploited through questions based upon it. It must be concise so that the pupil is not overburdened with reading and comprehension of the information itself, unless of course this is the deliberate intent. If it is intended to test higher abilities than recall of knowledge then the material used to present the information should either be unfamiliar in part at least to the pupils or be familiar material presented in an unfamiliar way. It should indicate what is the overall purpose of the set as a whole in order that as the pupils work through the questions they will know the general direction in which they are going. All the questions should use the material but will interact with it in different ways. For instance Questions 7 and 8 in the Physics example use the diagram much less directly than do Questions 1 and 2.

The following general guidelines should be borne in mind when setting a structured set of the kind illustrated.

1 The questions should in general be open ended and require short answers.
2 Within the set the questions should be easy to begin with and grow progressively more difficult. The degree of difficulty as in the example is often associated with demands for longer answers from the pupils. Do not, however, assume this to be automatically the case.
3 The answer to one question should not usually depend

on the pupil knowing the answer to an earlier one.

4 An appropriate space should be allowed on the question paper so that the pupils have a clear indication of how much they are expected to write.

5 Each question should be clearly designed to test a specific educational objective. In the example the skills which it is considered that the questions are testing have been listed in outline terms using the Bloom taxonomy. They would normally be expanded in relation to the subject involved, in this case Physics. It needs to be remembered also that the skills are defined in relation to the age group answering the questions in this case 15–16 year olds.

6 The set of questions should always be looked at by the writer through the eyes of those who are going to answer it (hence the importance of pretesting) and a marking scheme should be devised at the same time as the questions are written. This scheme should be detailed and an appropriate mark allocated for each point which is expected in the answers. With a finely structured set of questions and a detailed marking scheme a high degree of reliability in marking can be obtained.

The second example is taken from History. It is perfectly possible in History to use a set similar to the one illustrated for Physics based upon, say, photographs or extracts from source material. History also makes use of the single structured question, based sometimes, as in this example, upon a brief selection of material.

'Even before the end of hostilities it had become clear to a number of thoughtful people that Europe's political compartmentalisation far from being a sign of vitality and a guarantee of full opportunity for each country was a source of enfeeblement and decline.'

(Quoted in *'Europe is my Country'*, P. Wales)

'I look forward to a United States of Europe ... I trust that the European family may act unitedly.'

(Winston Churchill, 1942)

'We see opposite us on the mainland of Europe a large group comparable in size only to the United States and the Soviet Union, and as its power increases so will its political influence.'

(Edward Heath, 1962)

With regard to these three quotations write a continuous essay on the movement towards European unity, including the following points:
    1   Comment on the reasons for a United Europe.
    2   What were the early attempts towards United European policy?
    3   How was the European Economic Community set up?
    4   Trace Britain's relations with the EEC up to 1964.

Here the intention is to provide the pupils with definite guidelines for the writing of the answer to the extent of setting down potential although not exclusive paragraph headings. Once again the framework which this suggests to the pupils not only aids them but makes it more likely that those marking the answers will have a reasonable basis for comparison, although the greater length of the responses here will inevitably create more problems.

Open ended questions

The use of the words 'open ended' implies two things, first, that those answering the questions decide what to include and what not to include in their answers and, second, that no precise limits are normally set in the questions themselves as to length or style of answer. They thus deliberately provide little in the way of guidance to the respondent. Both in the classroom and in public secondary examinations the half-hour essay has been the most frequently used open ended question. When as happens on occasion longer or shorter answers are asked for, then the time allowance is adjusted accordingly.

The essay and extended written responses in general provide the most appropriate vehicle for assessing command of language and for demonstrating ability to analyse, to argue, to synthesise and to reflect. It is of course perfectly possible to demonstrate and hence to assess these orally, although whatever the medium used they are very much abilities which develop with maturity. In practice, however, the essay at the secondary level has been used much more frequently to assess basic knowledge and understanding of a topic. While one cannot argue or reflect without adequate knowledge and understanding there is no doubt that there are more effective ways than essays of testing these latter abilities. This has indeed been recognised in current assessment practice by the use of a much greater variety of written questions of the type described in this chapter. This change of emphasis has also encouraged experimentation with the setting and marking of open ended questions.

The main problem in setting open ended questions has always been how to make the intent explicit in a situation where the principal reason for using such questions is to provoke open-ended responses. To achieve this more attention needs to be paid to the 'lead' word in the question. If we ask pupils to *'Describe* the causes of the American Civil War' then it is unreasonable to expect them to do more than just this. If we want them to *'account for'* the causes or *'explain'* them or *'estimate* their relative importance' then the wording of the question should make this clear in specific terms. This again underlines the importance of the first general commandment for question writers.

Two recent approaches to the problem of how to use open ended questions to the best advantage have been the 'open book examination' and the 'prepared essay'.

In an open book examinaton pupils are allowed to bring books into the examination and on occasion notes upon these books, which they may use in answering the questions. Although in theory this approach may be used in relation to any kind of written or indeed oral question, in practice its feasibility is limited to open ended written questions. Restrictions may be laid upon the number of books, or upon the editions used. On occasion, for example with an atlas a specific edition may be prescribed for all pupils. Experience with open book examinations has emphasised two points. First, that different kinds of questions need to be asked: questions that require pupils to use the books and not merely to refer to them as if they were a form of licensed crib. Second, as with all forms of assessment, this approach benefits some pupils at the expense of others. Here it is the pupil with a good memory who can organise and plan who benefits – very often indeed these are the students who will not need to refer to the books. These may be legitimate qualities to assess but this may not be the way to assess them.

In the prepared essay pupils are given some time in advance of the examination itself, either the topic upon which the question will be asked or the actual question itself. Usually if the topic only is given then notes can be brought into the examination and used when answering the question. If the question itself is known in advance then usually nothing may be brought in. Although this approach can relieve pupils of examination tension and can encourage systematic preparatory work, it places a very heavy premium upon memorisation.

It is of course perfectly possible to ensure both with the 'open book examination' and the 'prepared essay' that pupils have understood what they have written by giving them an oral upon it. This, however, as will be seen in the next chapter can be extremely time-consuming. It is probably better to make use of both these approaches within the context of a course work folder as examples of the range of a pupil's work over a period of time. In assessing response to English Literature for example it is desirable not only that a variety of literature should elicit responses, e.g. drama, poetry, the novel and so on but also that the responses should be produced under different conditions, sometimes with assistance, sometimes without, sometimes under time constraints, sometimes not and so on. The project may also turn out to be a better vehicle for exploiting the principal benefits of the prepared essay.

The marking of open ended questions has always been as significant a problem as their setting. Indeed the majority of studies devoted to the essay in recent years have been concerned with marker reliability. These, while necessary, have tended to obscure the fact that marker unreliability starts with badly constructed and unclear questions. To concentrate solely upon marking is rather like buying fire extinguishers after the blaze has got well under way. There are two basic approaches to the marking of open ended questions: analytic and impression. Analytic marking requires the production and use of mark schemes which may be more or less detailed according to the nature of the subject and the needs of those conducting the assessment. Where large numbers of markers are employed then the mark scheme will be used as the basis for co-ordination. The closer those using it approximate to the interpretation laid down by the agency organising the marking the more reliable they are considered to be. Analytic marking thus represents an attempt to iron out differences in advance and hence to secure as much objectivity as possible, although it must be remembered that the interpretation against which the degree of agreement is measured is itself the result of a subjective decision.

Impression marking requires as its name implies those marking the answers to read them quickly without benefit of a mark scheme and to record their impression in the form of a mark or a grade. It is normal when impression marking is being used on any scale for it to be undertaken by several markers whose impressions are then averaged. Impression marking thus tries to harness the essential subjectivity of marking open ended questions by making the mark or grade awarded a reflection of an average judgment. Investigations into multiple marking suggest that three is the number of markers which maximises the benefits without imposing unacceptable demands in terms of time and cost. Logistic considerations have however made most large scale examinations employ only two when using this approach. Another variant of multiple marking occurs when all the answers to any one question are marked by the same person. Here it is the whole paper and not an individual question which is being multiply marked, the result being the sum of marks awarded for all questions are not the average of the mark given for each question. A weakness of multiple impression marking results from the fact that little has been done to identify the causes of differences between markers. Are there, for example, those whose marks for English essays are largely determined by the mechanics of the answer, e.g. spelling and punctuation? Are there others for whom the main consideration is the use of language and the range of vocabulary employed? If markers could be type-cast in this way even into fairly broad categories then it would be possible to put together those who were differently motivated. If this is not done then the average judgment resulting from a multiple impression mark may be nothing more than a repetition of similar judgments.

The previous paragraphs have talked of analytic and impression marking as if they were completely separate. In practice of course experienced teachers in the classroom working as they so often have to on their own (departmental marking is a possibility in English but is not often undertaken) employ a mixture of both, using one as a yardstick against which to judge the other. However, the reliability of their own marking or the method to use is probably not the main problem that faces teachers marking open ended responses from their own pupils. It is rather the extent to which they wittingly or unwittingly take into account or wish to take into account in the award they give, their knowledge of these same pupils – knowledge which is not available to a public examining body. This once again underlines the need for co-operative activity between teachers in assessment.

Chapter three

Techniques of assessment II

Introduction to oral assessment

Most of what has been said of a general nature under written assessment in the previous chapter, particularly in relation to structure, applies equally to oral assessment. There are, however, certain differences. Questions become much more alive when spoken and in consequence the personalities of those who actually ask the questions have to be taken into account. Because oral assessment is extensively used in languages which are foreign to those involved, problems such as accent and pronunciation are encountered. Oral assessment, moreover, plays a more important part in the testing of comprehension than does written assessment and a different range of skills is therefore brought into consideration. In view of the fact that most people spend more of their life in speaking than they do in writing or in practical activities, the oral is still very much under-used, both in teaching and in assessment and is limited to a narrow range of subjects, notably English and foreign languages. Attempts to widen its usage in assessment, in for example, Chemistry, Geography and History have only served to underline the difficulties involved, although fruitful work in the latter two subjects has been carried out in association with project work.

To a greater extent than other techniques oral assessment can be directed at specific skills and in consequence of this the methods used are on occasions highly artificial. Before looking at some specific areas one other general point needs emphasis, namely that oral assessment will involve the teacher more directly in the assessment process than written assessment. While it is perfectly possible in an external oral examination for people from outside the school to come in to assess, it is far more natural and less time-consuming for the pupils' own teacher to be involved. Under such circumstances the principal concern of the external agency will lie with sample moderation in order to establish and maintain comparable standards between schools. This means that teachers will need to concentrate upon the techniques of conducting orals. If one sees an apparently effortless performance by a teacher in this field one can be certain that it is the product of much hard work and no little skill. It is, moreover, a skill as with so much in assessment whose acquisition will be of benefit to the teacher as a teacher and not simply as an assessor. No two oral assessors work in the same way and a great deal can be gained from watching experienced colleagues in action. The key point is to avoid making the test one of confrontation. This is much more likely to occur in an oral examination because of the personal interaction that takes place between the assessor and the assessed. For this reason also it is impossible to set down hard and fast rules and what follows, therefore, are merely suggestions which may be found helpful. Everything possible should be done to set the student at ease. One way of doing this is to introduce the topic gradually through personal discussion based perhaps on previously seen material such as a picture or diary. The assessor should also try, wherever possible, to build upon the pupil's experience. In general, questions which require a straight 'yes' or 'no' should be avoided and questions which permit a more extended answer used instead. The assessor should at all costs avoid sarcasm and the use of words which are likely to be misunderstood by the pupil.

In constrast to the section of written questions, where specific points were brought out through consideration of different forms of questioning, the treatment here will be largely subject-based and the points will be brought out under the four headings of English, Foreign Languages, Other Subjects and Group Discussion.

Oral assessment in English

In its English S Syllabus for 1975 the Southern Regional
Examinations Board for the CSE states that the ability to
communicate ideas and sustain conversation, clear and distinct
articulation and lively and expressive delivery will be looked
for in the Oral Test. These general points suggest three possible
areas for assessment, Technical Excellence, Ability to Communicate and the Human Factor. It is relatively easy to suggest
and spell out the qualities one would look for and hope to find
among pupils of secondary school age in these three areas.
Under Technical Excellence there would be such factors as
clarity of enunciation, fluency, quality of voice, extent and
range of vocabulary, correct emphasis and intonation and
freedom from serious grammatical error. Under Ability to
Communicate there would be the ability to follow, develop
and maintain an argument and the ability to convey ideas to
another person in a clear and coherent manner. Under the
Human Factor there would be such things as natural flow of
ideas, evidence of a sense of humour, signs of originality and
sincerity and signs of interest in other individuals and in the
world around the pupil. Decisions as to whether to include or
to exclude certain factors are, of course, subjective ones by the
individual or the group preparing the courses and the criteria
for assessing them. It is not always easy, however, to decide
under which heading to place a particular factor or ability, nor
is it possible to avoid repetition. What, for example, is the
difference between 'fluency' and 'natural flow of ideas'?
However precise one tries to be there remains a degree of
generality in most statements of criteria until they are specifically tied down to a particular group of pupils and to a
particular subject. The phrases 'clear and coherent manner'
and 'freedom from serious grammatical error' for example are
quite rightly open to differing interpretations in the light of
those whom one teaches. Where an external agency is involved
it is the prime task of that agency to try and secure agreement
about the meaning of such terms through a process of
moderation, and on occasions this may mean that the

wishes of individual schools and teachers have to be over-ridden.

The remarks made in the last half of the preceding paragraph draw attention indirectly to the problem of weighting which is much less easy to determine than the criteria for assessment. Weighting ought to reflect the views held about the teaching of the subject by those who decide what that weighting shall be.

In a school this will be staff and occasionally the pupils; in an examining board it will normally be the subject panels, acting as representatives of those who enter candidates for the board's examinations. A heavy weighting given to technical excellence in English for example should not only reflect but be reflected in a different approach to the teaching of the subject, as compared with a heavy weighting upon the ability to communicate in a lively and interesting manner. The same would be true of French where different weightings for oral and written skills ought to reflect different, although equally legitimate, teaching approaches. One of the reasons why pupils on occasion put up startlingly different performances upon the examinations of different public examining boards is that the examinations are either assessing different abilities or the same abilities differently weighted. Inevitably these differences favour some pupils at the expense of others.

The third area mentioned earlier, the Human Factor, presents particular difficulties as far as the determination of weighting for assessment is concerned. For many teachers it is the most important area of all, but it is highly subjective and difficult to define. One knows very well in real life that different people have very different senses of humour. How can we determine originality in a 16-year-old? Is it not easier to say that pupils are sincere when they are defending an issue of which society approves such as campaigns against pollution rather than one of which it disapproves such as apartheid? This area of attitudes, the affective domain of the Bloom taxonomies, is one in which the requirements of reliable assessement may be at odds with outcomes of the curriculum which teachers think to be of great importance. This is a matter which will be further discussed at the end of this chapter. As well as being a reflection of the relative importance attached to the skills being assessed the weighting should itself be reflected in the techniques used to assess them and in the time allocated to each part of the assessment. It is unfair, as has already been said, to subject pupils to particularly demanding techniques or to ask them to take considerable time over work for which only 10 per cent of the available marks are awarded. Yet this is often done. A project occupying some two terms of work is weighted at 20 per cent or less in many public examinations whilst a written paper lasting 2 hours is weighted at 80 per cent.

The problem of artificiality is the great problem associated with the assessment of languages at the secondary level, both mother tongue and foreign, although it is more acute with the latter. The main reason for this is the difficulty that most 16-year-olds have in sustaining a free-flowing conversation within the kind of framework imposed by assessed courses of study in these areas of the curriculum. This is, of course, as much a criticism of the courses of study as it is of the methods of assessment. This difficulty has caused the approaches to oral assessment, again perhaps more so in foreign languages than in the mother tongue, to oscillate between two extremes, the one relatively unstructured and the other highly structured. In general the emphasis at the present time is towards a structured approach. In English the techniques most frequently used are:

1 Reading a piece of prose, poetry or drama;
2 Reading from a book which the pupil has enjoyed;
3 A short talk which is the outcome of the pupil's own experience;
4 Answering questions asked by an examiner or other members in a group situation;
5 The individual interview.

Of these techniques, reading has been largely eliminated in recent years as a technique in its own right and is now more often used as an introduction to conversation either to provide material for that conversation or to put pupils at their ease. The individual interview still remains the staple diet of much oral assessment in English but it has been modified substantially in recent years in order to overcome its major disadvantage, namely the confrontation situation between pupil and interviewer which it introduces. In consequence the conversation can easily become stilted and one-sided although this can be minimised when the examiner is the candidate's own teacher. The most commonly used method, therefore, today is the structured conversation in which the pupil is provided with a framework within which to operate either through the use of selected material or by concentration in the conversation upon known areas of interest in work, sport or hobbies or upon work done in class.

A skilled teacher can use this framework to permit very considerable flexibility and thus enable pupils to show themselves to the best advantage. Most oral assessment in English is still individual assessment. Group assessment which will be considered later is more prevalent in the Humanities and courses in the general area of 'social studies'.

It will have been noted that nowhere in this section so far has any mention been made of accent. Oral assessment is now not regarded as an elocution test and regional characteristics ought not to be, and rarely are, penalised in practice so long as they do not inhibit comprehension. A more difficult problem can, of course, arise when a pupil being assessed suffers from a speech defect such as a stutter. All that can be done here is try everything to set such a pupil at ease. It must, however, be remembered that what is being tested is oral competence and that the pupil has to be assessed upon this. Unfortunately in public examinations we give global grades for complete subjects, rather than a description of performance in different areas of these subjects. In consequence a pupil's overall grade in English could be affected by a poor oral performance. If the oral were to be described or even graded independently of the written work then only the oral result would be affected and this would help pupils who suffer from minor speech defects.

Oral assessment in foreign languages

Although certain of the criteria that are used in the oral assessment of English come into play in the oral assessment of foreign languages (for practical purposes it will be assumed that the language considered here is French) there are important differences. Accent and pronunciation become more significant and far more emphasis is placed upon the ability to comprehend what is being said. The assessment tends to become more artificial and structured than in the mother tongue because the difficulties of holding an extended conversation are greater. In consequence the 'examiner's' role also becomes even more important and exacting and he or she thus needs more support from the framework of the assessment. This greater use of structure reflects what occurs in the teaching situation where the spoken skills of French are often taught as 'drill' skills. There is also a much greater use of taped material for assessment purposes in French than is the case in English. It is indeed very important that those engaged in oral and also aural assessment know how to operate tape recording equipment. Faulty recording can be very damaging to the assessment of pupils. The skills most frequently tested at the secondary level in French are comprehension (usually the most heavily weighted), pronunciation, intonation and phrasing, the range of ideas (more questionable perhaps at the secondary level than the others) and accuracy of expression and extent and range of vocabulary. For testing these skills there is a wide range of techniques in current use; indeed it is arguable that too many techniques are being used. Much assessment in oral French is open to the criticism of being too fragmented with the result that pupils never get their teeth into any one activity and there is in consequence considerable danger of over-testing certain skills and under-testing others. These techniques are as follows:

1 Reading aloud;
2 Exposés with little or no prompting from the 'examiner';
3 List of prepared questions;

4 Picture based tests either single or linked pictures.

In all these there is very little interaction between examiner and examinee, that is to say it is a formal speech situation.

5 Free general conversation;
6 Conversation based upon a prepared subject; this can sometimes follow on from the exposé;
7 Role-playing or assignments in which the assessor acts a part corresponding to a role assigned to the examinee.

These last three are reciprocal speech situations. All these methods can be structured more or less severely according to the needs of both pupil and teacher although it will be noted that some of them are inherently more structured than others, compare for example the list of prepared questions with the free general conversation.

We tend on occasions to assume that marking problems are exclusively associated with written questions. This is far from the truth; problems of evaluating the answer to any question relate more to the nature of the question and the way it is framed than they do to the medium used in its presentation. As with written questions so with oral, greater structure can permit a more comprehensive breakdown of marks and help to minimise, although not eliminate, marker unreliability. The more open-ended the response the question is designed to evoke, the more difficult it is to provide other than guidelines for its marking. The points made earlier in relation to the marking of written questions are equally relevant here.

Oral assessment in other subjects

As far as secondary school examinations are concerned the one major study reported of oral assessment replacing other methods of assessment in a subject normally not associated with oral work, in this case Chemistry, is to be found in Schools Council Examinations Bulletin No. 21. The conclusions of its authors are of interest as they show both the advantages and difficulties of introducing oral assessment on a wider scale as a replacement for other methods. These were as follows:

(a) Oral assessment had 'reasonably' high reliability and validity. (The word 'reasonably' would seem to require amplification.)

(b) There were considerable administrative problems and the process was very time-consuming.

(c) There was a healthy backwash (some authorities have coined the word 'beneficence' to describe this) resulting from the inevitable classroom discussion that oral work induced.

(d) It appealed to pupils whose ability in the subject was limited and who disliked written examinations.

The authors did not find nervousness a limiting factor but underlined the importance of the pupil/teacher or examiner/candidate relationship. They believed that orals in subjects such as Chemistry had two important functions, first as a means of assessment in its own right and second, as a means of moderating work already undertaken. There is in these remarks a clear conflict between beneficial educational considerations and less beneficial administrative considerations. The crux, assuming a reasonable economic climate, must lie in the answer to the question 'Are the likely advantages sufficiently important to outweigh the likely disadvantages?' In order to answer this question it is necessary to do more than simply compare different techniques. The relationship of what is proposed for assessment to the technique used is the crucial issue.

One possible use of oral assessment upon which the authors of SCEB No. 21 do not lay great stress is that of a support or complement to other forms of assessment. This is different from its role as a moderating instrument although it may help in this respect. Some of the possibilities here are illustrated by a study currently being undertaken by the University of London School Examinations Council and the Middlesex CSE

Board as part of the 16+ feasibility/development exercises. This study investigated, amongst other things, five approaches to the use of oral assessment in History, as follows:

1. An oral based upon a project;
2. A 2–3 minute talk based upon a specific area of the syllabus followed by a general discussion on the course as a whole;
3. A structured oral of the kind described in SCEB No. 21 using a map on the Treaty of Versailles;
4. A completely unstructured oral about the course in general;
5. A semi-structured oral using a variety of stimulus material.

The merits and demerits of these various approaches will be brought up in the report upon the study which should provide valuable guidelines and suggestions for other subjects. Approach 1, however, would seem to offer considerable possibilities for profitable use. A practical exercise in handicraft, an individual study, a laboratory notebook, a geography field work exercise, for example, would all seem to benefit by the addition of oral assessment. Its use would introduce another dimension and make it possible to reinforce or modify impressions gained from looking at the written or practical work of pupils. An oral would also enable the pupils' understanding of the work, of which there may very well be a great deal, to be evaluated. Furthermore, an oral could provide opportunities for pupils to convey some idea of the enjoyment they have gained from their work. Many youngsters aged between 11 and 19 are able to put over their interests and enjoyment more readily orally than they can in writing. As always such oral assessment will place a heavy burden upon the person conducting it, a burden different from that imposed by its use in English and French. When the oral is based upon a particular piece of work, that work has first to be read or scrutinised in order that a range of suitable questions can be devised. To these questions will be added some more general questions relating to the subject or the area from which the work is taken. Additionally those assessing the work should be ready to take advantage of any opportunities offered by pupils to explore relevant areas of interest while not forgetting on occasion the need to cut down on irrelevance and to avoid 'red herrings'.

Oral assessment of group discussion

A feature of recent courses in Social Studies and the Humanities has been the emphasis placed upon discussion and this has focused attention upon the problem of assessing group work in general in an examination system which issues certificates to individuals. In an activity such as the planning, construction and carrying out of a survey it is possible to structure the scheme of work in order to ensure that all concerned carry out different aspects of the work at different times without distorting the scheme as a whole. In this way comparative judgments can be made about individuals at the end of the day. In group discussion this is impossible. One only has to envisage a typical staff meeting at a school to realise this and to appreciate the practical difficulties that face any kind of objective comparative assessment in such a situation not least that of time. There are really only two realistic approaches to the assessment of group discussion:

1 To involve the whole group, i.e. both pupils and teachers in the assessment process;
2 To involve a number of different people in assessing the group.

These assessors could each either be allocated an individual within the group, or a particular skill or quality to assess. If it was an individual then the judgment would be made about that individual upon an agreed range of skills. If it was a skill then performance upon that skill would be assessed for all the individuals in the group.

These procedures could be used upon either live or

recorded discussions. If a recording is used it ought wherever possible to be provided by a videotape.

A tape recording would reveal little of the subleties of group interaction which, while they may complicate the process of assessment, are an essential element in the dynamics of discussion.

One interesting experiment in the assessment of group discussion has been undertaken by John Miller of Blakelaw School, Newcastle upon Tyne in a course based upon the Schools Council Humanities Project. Miller identified three broad areas into which pupil comment might fall namely:

1 The processes of debate;
2 The nature of evidence;
3 Value judgments and personal positions.

Within each of these areas possible pupil contributions were identified and each was given a positive and negative description which in turn could be given a numerical rating. For example, under the nature of the evidence we might find a positive/negative rating such as:

Positive: Shows a preference for argument sustained by logic; questions prejudiced attitudes; queries hearsay evidence.

Negative: Adopts a prejudiced position unsupported by evidence; refuses to weigh counter-evidence; quotes and accepts unverifiable evidence.

This could be developed if desired into, say, a five point scale which indicated degrees of positiveness or negativeness. The points could be assigned numbers 1 to 5 or letters A to E and used as a set of more detailed criteria against which to assess pupils' contributions. Similar scales could be developed in the other areas.

The reader may well query whether teachers, let alone pupils, can acquire the necessary expertise to assess discussion in this way. Experience, however, in the use of interaction analysis in teacher training suggests that student teachers can readily acquire the ability to record objectively comments and activities whilst acting as observers. This is an essential preliminary to assessment of the kind proposed by Miller. A group of pupils could be shown a videotape of a discussion involving say twelve people and be asked first of all to record the number of comments made by each of the participants. A surprisingly high level of agreement should be achieved fairly quickly. This can then be followed by a crude evaluation of each comment on a three point scale in relation to a single criterion (e.g. relevance to the topic being discussed) as a preliminary to the development of more elaborate criteria and more elaborate scales. The resulting information can then be used for assessing individual students. It can also be used, and in this lies its greatest value, in improving pupil perception of the requirements of a successful discussion and in monitoring the performance of the group chairman and his impact upon the pupils.

As with oral assessment technical competence in the use of the machinery involved is very important. The ease with which a football match can be followed on television is directly related to the skill of the camera operators. This applies equally to the videotaping of a group discussion.

Introduction to aural assessment

If oral assessment is under-used, aural assessment is by comparison almost non-existent. In public examinations it is only really used to any extent in Modern Languages although there have been encouraging developments recently in Music. In English the work of the University of Birmingham Oracy Project has been described in a recent publication *The Quality of Listening* by Wilkinson, Stratta and Dudley, and this may stimulate further work in this area. In any aural assessment the use of the correct register is particularly important. The language used must be appropriate to speech and also to the situation, for example, a BBC announcer would use neither cockney nor a very informal turn of phrase when reading the news. In general, dialogue will be found to provide the most useful basis for aural testing. Documentary passages are of little value, while a monologue should be confined to short factual utterances. A wide variety of material and of situations should ideally be used although this can pose a conflict between what is desirable for assessment purposes and what is practicable. For example, five dialogues of 50 words each may provide much better discrimination than one of 250 words. On the other hand they are likely to be much more demanding to construct. Here, as with all forms of testing, the need for co-operative activity and sound knowledge both of subject and testing techniques are essential. It goes without saying also that the quality of any recordings used must be of the highest level.

Aural assessment in foreign languages

In foreign languages the principal emphasis has been upon language for survival and the methods most commonly used for assessment have been highly structured, namely:

1 Vocabulary tests based upon pictures;
2 Appropriate rejoinder questions;
3 True/False statements based upon pictures or dialogues;
4 Who? What? Where? situations presented from everyday life;
5 More extended dialogues or narratives.

Objective items, mainly multiple choice with some true/false, have been used almost exclusively. The degree of comprehension is, of course, affected by the complexity of the situation as well as by the difficulty of the questions asked and the techniques of questioning used, although the three factors interlock to a considerable degree.

Aural assessment in music

One of the most interesting aural tests in current use in public examinations in Music is that of the New Zealand School Certificate. This is described in some detail in order to illustrate the possibilities of aural assessment in this area. The second of the objectives of the examination as a whole is to encourage aural perception. This is tested by means of a 45 minute aural perception test which carries 40 per cent of the total weighting. The remainder of the examination consists of a written paper which carries a 60 per cent weighting. Practical work is not formally assessed but pupil performance is recorded by teachers upon a practical record card which will be referred to in the practical section later in the chapter. There are seven parts to the aural perception test which are all contained upon a single record namely:

1 General Perception;
2 Dictation of Rhythm;
3 Dictation of Melody;
4 Recognition of Interval and Harmony;
5 Recognition of Timbres;
6 Recognition of Musical Styles, Textures and Forms;
7 Identification of Passages from among the works prescribed for listening.

The whole test is answered by the pupils in answer booklets which they are required to annotate or complete according to given instructions.

The titles of tests 4, 5, 6 and 7 indicate fairly clearly their nature, but the first three are less obvious and are hence described in more detail. In the general perception test, Test 1, the candidates are given in their answer booklets a printed single- or two- stave unbarred score. The music concerned is then played five times and the candidates are asked to fill in all or some of the following: time signatures and bar lines, pace and alteration of pace, phrase marks and dynamics and the point reached in the performance. In Test 2, dictation of rhythm, the candidates are asked to write down the rhythm only of a four bar tune which begins at the first beat of the bar. The tune is played through once, then the first half is played twice and then the whole tune is played through three times. There are 20-second pauses between playings. The candidates are also provided with the speed of the beat. In Test 3, dictation of melody, the candidates are asked to write down a melody of not more than four bars after being given on several occasions as in Test 2 the rhythmic pattern and key signature.

Aural assessment in English

The authors of the *Quality of Listening* identify four elements in any communication:

1 The person making the communciation;
2 The person to whom it is addressed;
3 The topic referred to in the communication;
4 The context of the communication

Assessment can of course be directed to any of these elements considered either on its own or in combinations with any or all of the others. The authors also underline the marked differences that exist between written and spoken accounts of the same topic; for example, the repetition that takes place in speech makes an oral account much longer. Differences such as these need to be taken into account when assessing aurals.

The Birmingham Oracy Unit developed batteries of tests for use at three different age levels, 10–11, 13–14 and 17–18. That for the 13–14-year-olds was designed to test:

1 Content;
2 Contextual constraint;
3 Phonology;
4 Register;
5 Relationship.

The nature of the range of the techniques employed, all of which break new ground, will be illustrated by reference to the testing of contextual constraint and register. The basic principle used in testing the first of these was to omit a sentence from a communication and ask the pupil to supply it from a number of given alternatives (usually three) which were listed in the answer booklets. This is only possible if the words before and after the omission are supplied. A telephone conversation interrupted by interference provided one way of doing this. The method used to test register was to introduce an alien phrase into a passage otherwise spoken consistently in a single register. Many contrasts between registers can be made as for example:

Technical	—	Non-technical
Formal	—	Informal
Written	—	Spoken
Impersonal	—	Personal
Rational	—	Emotional
Public	—	Private

These tests and those in the Music examination illustrate one practical matter that arises in aural testing, namely the need to repeat the background material used, whether it be a speech or a piece of music on several occasions in order to avoid over-emphasising pure memorization.

Another issue of importance raised by some of the techniques used in oral as well as aural assessment is that of transfer. Are pupils, for example, who do well in the kinds of modern language tests described earlier likely to survive better on a holiday in France or Germany than those who do badly? The question of transfer is, of course, not confined to any one form of aural assessment but the more artificial the assessment technique used the more starkly it is likely to be posed. Artificiality is not only a question of technique but also of division of function. This draws attention once again to Hogben's fourth point (*Journal of Curriculum Studies* for May 1973) which was referred to in the first chapter, in the discussion upon objectives, namely that in translating broad curricular goals into more specific language we should make sure that the sum of the objectives faithfully reflects the full intention of the original goals which gave them birth. The more closely classroom and assessment practice can be married the more likely is the degree of artificiality in the assessment situation to be reduced. This of itself will not solve the problem of transfer but it ought to help limit the size of jump from the classroom to real life.

Introduction to practical assessment

In the two sections, written and oral, so far considered communication has taken the form of question and response. In this section communication most frequently takes the form of problem and solution. The posing of the problem ought to aim at creating a situation in which those being assessed can demonstrate their ability to find and justify solutions and their mastery of the relevant skills. The problem may, of course, have no one correct solution or indeed any solution at all.

Although there is a wide variety of approaches to the assessment of practical work in current use, these can be classified for convenience under three broad headings:

Set piece practical exercises;
Continuous assessment of practical skills;
Project work.

Although the need to define what is being assessed as a preliminary to assessing it is only referred to explicitly under the third of these headings, it is as necessary to the assessment of all practical work as to any other kind of assessment. As has been indicated earlier in the book relatively little emphasis will be given here to physical skills, although several of these, for example co-ordination between hand and eye, are essential requirements of laboratory work in Science. As such they might be included in assessment programmes in this area. The assessment of physical skills, however, presents problems particularly within the framework of a norm referenced public examinations system. It is far better in this area to lay down criteria of mastery as a basis upon which to determine levels of performance than to be concerned solely with a comparison of these levels as a basis for grading. The establishment of criteria of mastery is, of course, done in many school sports where standards are awarded to pupils in various events. These standards can be adjusted to take account of different ages and physical developments and can be lowered or raised in order to act either as a spur or a pat on the back.

Set piece practical exercises

Overwhelmingly, these set exercises take the form of written instructions to which the student responds in practical terms by doing something. Occasionally oral instructions are given or the situation may be presented pictorially in the form say of a piece of music which the pupil is asked to play. The written questions or exercises can take a wide variety of forms and a number of these will now be illustrated.

There is first of all the written question which asks for a largely or exclusively written response. That response, however, cannot be correctly given unless the relevant practical work has been undertaken during the course. An example of such a question follows:

(a) The molecular kinetic theory suggests a model to help in the understanding of the physical behaviour of materials. With respect to gases what does this model assume about (i) the nature of a molecule, (ii) the movement of a molecule?
Describe an experiment to illustrate osmosis.
(b) Describe the structure at room temperature of (i) sodium chloride, and (ii) methane.
Give reasons why you would consider it incorrect to use the term 'molecule' in describing the structure of sodium chloride but not in describing the structure of methane.

(Joint Matriculation Board, Physical Science (Ordinary Level) June 1975)

Here written answers only are required although the experiment asked for in part (b) could be illustrated by means of a diagram or diagrams. The principal disadvantage of such questions is that they provide no indication of the student's proficiency in the practical work upon which the answers are based. Written answers may describe very well how to mend a puncture in a bicycle tyre but that description will not indicate how neat or clumsy was the workmanship nor how long the tyre remained inflated after it had been repaired. In order to test these things – assuming that they are considered to be worth testing – it must be a requirement that the puncture is actually mended.

The kind of set piece exercise to which the previous question was in part a reaction is still, however, widely used, the following being a typical example:

> You are living in a flat with a friend and share the chores. It is your turn to cook the Sunday lunch and to clear up.
> Prepare, cook and serve an attractive three course lunch for two of you costing no more than £1. Launder the table-cloth, set the table and arrange some flowers. Clean the stainless steel cutlery you will use.
> (Southern Regional Examinations Board – Home Economics 1974)

Let us assume that this question was the sole practical assessment within a CSE Home Economics examination. This may appear unlikely but in fact practical work in public examinations in many subjects was assessed in this way not so long ago. The principal disadvantage of this approach is that the assessment takes no heed of the realities of practical work. It is in no sense a miniature but at best a fleeting impression. Even the best cooks have their bad days and their failures, and the gas pressure is not always constant. It is not surprising therefore that performance on tests of this kind does not tend to correlate highly with teacher estimates of pupils' practical ability. There are, moreover, substantial administrative difficulties in assessing large numbers of pupils in this way.

There are a number of ways in which these deficiencies can be minimised. First of all there is the allocation of adequate time. In the case of the Home Economics exercise this was as follows: Planning period – 2 hours; Preparation period – 1 hour; Examination period — 2½ hours. The comparison here with the prepared essay is revealing. This allocation probably represents a reasonable compromise between the requirements of a set piece examination and the nature of the situation in real life.

Art probably raises the question of time in its most extreme form. Whilst most Art examinations today place substantial emphasis upon work done throughout the course many retain as well an examination piece rather similar in conception to the medieval apprentice's 'master piece'. The questions used to stimulate such a piece are, however, very open-ended as for example, 'Very young children are fascinated by sound, bright colours and moving shapes. Make something appealing which will include at least two of these qualities' (SREB Art and Craft, 1974). The accompanying rubric to this question and others like it reads as follows:

The question paper will be issued to each candidate at least seven days before the date of the examination. They will have a choice of question and their response may take a two or three dimensional form. Preparatory work may be brought into the examination room.

The time allowed for the examination will normally be five hours in one school day. Where a candidate requires further time, work must be completed within the three weeks following the date of the examination.

Candidates may withdraw from the examination room at any time in order to get reference information and may retire as soon as they are satisfied that their work is complete.

It is clear that this kind of set exercise is a far cry from the Physical Science or Home Economics examples given earlier. The marking of subjective work such as Art also presents particular difficulties. These can best be resolved by group assessment on an impression basis. The marks or grades awarded by the group can either be averaged out or the highest and lowest marks or grades eliminated and an average taken of the remainder.

Techniques of assessment II

A second possible improvement would be to make this exercise one of a number of similar exercises. At one time alternative exercises were set from which either the pupil or the teacher was asked to choose one. On occasion the exercises were randomly allocated. More recently the tendency has been to set a number of exercises all of which are to be taken by all pupils over a period of say a year. This means that the practical assessment can be integrated into the course as a natural activity. It serves also to ease the administrative problems and ensures that all pupils are assessed on a wide range of practical activities.

This structuring of the course can, of course, be tightened as well as loosened. The Art example is about as loose as it possibly could be while remaining a set exercise. Many of the 'investigation' questions currently set in science practicals represent the other extreme. Take for example this half-hour exercise in Biology:

Tubes A, B, C, D, E and F contain colourless liquids.
(a) Pipette 2—3 drops of iodine in potassium iodide solution into tube A.
    Put a small piece of sample X into tube F which contains alcohol (ethanol) and shake at intervals. Then pour the liquid into tube B which contains water.
    Pipette 10 drops of Benedict's solution into tube C and boil for 1 minute in the water bath.
    Pipette 5 drops of standardised Bicarbonate Indicator into tube D and tube E. Invert to mix.
(b) Complete this table.

Tube	Change observed	Substance detected by the test
A		
B		
C		
D		
E		
F		

(c) What food substance should be added to those indicated in your table to provide a complete diet for a young mammal?

....

....

(d) Which of the tests are *not* food tests?

....

....

(SREB Biology S, 1974)

A more open investigation is equally possible as a set exercise as, for example, this in Human Biology:

The beaker labelled C contains a solution of two common foodstuffs. Carry out food tests to identify the two substances. Record all the tests you make, but there is no need to make other tests once you have positively identified the two substances.
Complete the table below:

Brief description of the test	Observations	Conclusions

[This table has been cut down in order to save space.]
(SREB Human Biology S 1974)

Enough illustrations have been provided to suggest that set practical exercises are in the main written questions which demand practical rather than written responses. As such they

75

can make use of every possible variety of structure. The structure used will condition the response and hence its marking. The Biology investigation would, for example, be accompanied by a detailed breakdown of marks while the Art would almost certainly be marked on a multiple-impression basis. As with all written questions, clarity of wording and the need to ensure that the pupils know exactly what is required of them are of paramount importance. The Home Economics exercise, for example, could be criticised for its failure to indicate the relative weighting to be given to planning, the preparation of the meal, costing, laundering, flower arrangement and cleaning all of which were requirements. The absence of any such indication could either lead to marking difficulties in the face of different responses or to the establishment of the kind of mark scheme which ought to have been built into the question when it was set.

It is hoped also that the examples used will have underlined the major disadvantage of the set exercise for the assessment of practical work, namely its artificiality. It is this more than anything else that has led to an increased use of internal assessment.

Continuous assessment of practical skills

Internal assessment of practical work can only be carried out by those who teach the pupils being assessed and it should, if it is to provide a fair reflection of performance, be undertaken over a substantial period of time, say a year. This means that from the outset there must be a clear idea of what is to be assessed. The discussion earlier in the book upon continuous assessment would seem to suggest that a programme of this kind will in practice be subject to periodic assessment. This in turn implies the need to maintain careful and detailed records. Definition and the maintenance of records are then the key elements and it is upon these two topics that this section will concentrate.

The principal problem here is to determine how detailed

the definition needs or ought to be. Some idea of possible levels of generality in definition can be provided by looking at two examples. The first is taken from an unpublished paper upon assessment in science by Dr J. Duffey, while the second consists of proposals put forward by the Joint Matriculation Board for the internal assessment of practical skills in their GCE A level Alternative Chemistry syllabus.

1   Duffey suggests that practical skills in Science can be assessed globally in relation to the following criteria which he embodies in a five point scale, namely:

A Very neat and skilful with his hands. Attracted by any tasks involving mechanical intricacies, e.g. taking a lock to pieces or repairing bicycles. Good craftsman, sensible in handling and using apparatus.

B Quite capable with apparatus. Likes practical work and is sensible in using instruments. Not averse to craft hobbies but not single minded.

C Not outstanding in any way. Reasonably good manipulation of apparatus, handles tools and instruments competently but without skill or enthusiasm.

D Rather lacking in practical skills. Set up apparatus insecurely. Not very interested in craft hobbies. Needs a lot of help in the laboratory.

E Very clumsy and ham-fisted in using tools and instruments. No interest in practical toys or hobbies.

It will be seen that this scale is based upon descriptions of imaginary pupils who have been given characteristics relating to different levels of competency in practical work.

It is worth noting incidentally that the scale includes some consideration of pupil attitudes to practical work. These characteristics have been developed into a very generalised scale, which probably represents the most general level at which definition is likely to be useful for assessment purposes. At most it can be used to provide a fairly wide overall judgment of a pupil's practical ability since it is inevitably lacking in detail. The scale of course contains within it numerous skills or attributes which are capable of development into scales of their own, e.g. skills in observation, manipulative skills, qualities such as persistence. Indeed Duffey himself has suggested similar five point scales in some of these areas: that proposed for persistence is illustrated later in this chapter.

2   The other example is not a scale but simply a statement of what the JMB considers should form the basis for the assessment of practical skills in the subject concerned. The different ways in which this statement has been elaborated illustrates the problem facing any external agency which wishes to introduce internal assessment as a part of its examination programme. If too little detail is provided then it may be difficult to secure agreement between those engaged in the assessment. If there is too much detail then restrictions may be placed upon teachers' ability to develop their own courses in their own ways. If this occurs then a feature which led to the rejection of the set exercise will have been reintroduced. The JMB which has had more experience of large-scale internal assessment than any other public examining body is far from satisfied that it has found the best solution even assuming there is one. Continuous experimentation is taking place as witness its recent proposals in Domestic Science and Geography both at A level. The expansion of the proposals for Chemistry will serve however to illustrate this variety adequately.

Five qualities are listed for assessment, namely

A Skill in observation and accurate recording of observation;
B Ability to interpret practical experience;
C Ability to plan and carry out experiments;
D The possession of appropriate manipulative skills;
E Attitudes to practical work.

Qualities A, B and C are simply expanded through a brief written description designed to draw teachers' attention to the kinds of practical work that would enable their pupils to demonstrate the qualities concerned. There is a thin line between this approach and suggesting specific experiments which some teachers would inevitably regard as prescriptive but the JMB have so far resisted demands for further detail.

Qualities D and E are expanded in different ways. Under D (manipulative skills) a list is provided of 14 possible skills which practical work in science can encourage. No attempt is made to weight these skills or emphasise one at the expense of another.

Quality E (attitudes to practical work) is expanded by giving three more specific sub-headings upon which teachers are asked to concentrate namely 'willingness to co-operate in the normal routine of a laboratory', 'persistence and resourcefulness' and 'enthusiasm'. Each of these is itself briefly expanded: for example under 'persistence and resourcefulness' it states, 'This will involve the student's willingness to work unaided on given problems and his ability to see them through to a meaningful solution'.

The nature of the definitions provided will to a considerable extent determine the approaches adopted for assessment purposes. This interaction between definition and assessment can best be illustrated by referring again to the two examples.

1   Any remarks made about the Duffey scale apply in general terms to all scales of this kind. As has already been suggested in the example given the information gained through its use can only be of a very general kind. More specific scales would provide more specific information. Basically a scale provides a framework against which pupils can be rated either on a once for all basis or as here periodically. Each pupil in class or in a school can be compared against the framework and can be allocated as a result one of the points on the scale. These points in their turn can be quantified in whatever way the user wishes in order to obtain a mark, a grade, or a rank order. Pupil progress over a course can also be presented in relation to the scale in a variety of ways, as shown in Figure 2.

The letters A, B, C, etc. represent the descriptions on the scale against which the pupil has been judged, in this case monthly. Readers can readily think of other ways of presenting this information and can also appreciate that its presentation does not in any way solve the problem of what value to give to different performances particularly when it is necessary, as it is in a public examination, to give a global evaluation in the form of a grade at the end of the course.

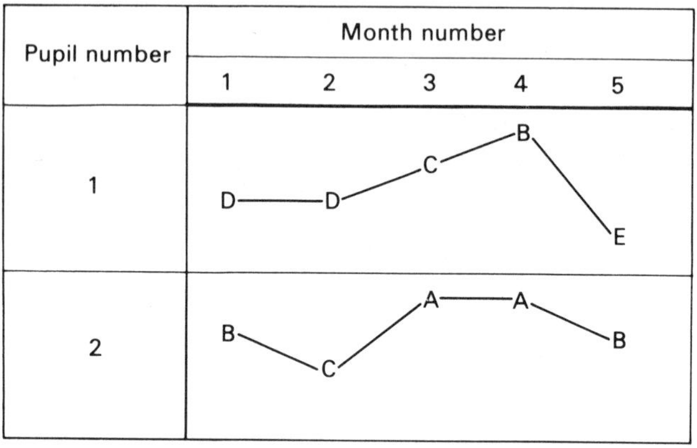

FIGURE 2

2   The last point in the previous paragraph is a problem that the JMB Chemistry scheme has to tackle since A level results are issued in terms of single grades for the examination as a whole. In the Chemistry scheme a very large degree of flexibility is given to the teacher in terms both of how to assess and when to assess. The scheme requires each teacher to assess each of the five qualities upon a ten point scale. The sum of these assessments will provide an overall mark for each student expressed out of 50. The total marks will thus provide an overall rank order for each class of pupils as well as indicating qualitative differences between them. By way of illustration the ten point scale used for quality B 'to interpret practical experience' is as follows:

> 10 – 9   Good appreciation of data, appreciation of error and limitation of experiment. Knows when to obtain additional results. Good analytical approach. Good appreciation of apparatus

required, scale of experiment, etc. Ability to calculate accurately results from experimental data. Good written and, where appropriate, oral appreciation of results and appreciation of variables. The ability to relate the whole of his practical experience to particular problems.

8 – 7   Data appreciated. Adequate analysis of procedure and analysis of error. Method of calculation correct but liable to minor errors.

6 – 5   Data appreciated. Some help required. Some progress in calculation.

4 – 3   Little understanding of the relevance of data. Difficulty in handling data and carrying out calculations. Requires assistance in interpreting results and applying experience. Offers no comment on chemically stupid answers.

2 – 1   Needs a great deal of help at all stages.

It will be noted that the criteria which form the scale have been expressed in ranges of two marks. It was felt that a single mark range would have required teachers to satisfy distinctions which were too fine for practical definition. Teachers are required to apply the criteria on the basis of their own standards and the evidence provided by their pupils. While for the whole JMB entry marks of 10 or 1 will be found it is not necessary for any one school to use the complete range of marks. The JMB recommends that teachers arrive at the final assessment for any one quality as a result of assessments carried out during the course, the final mark awarded being the average of the marks awarded for those assessments. The total mark upon which the overall ranking is based is, therefore, obtained by summing the final marks awarded for each of the five qualities.

It is fairly obvious that procedures such as these require the maintenance of detailed records by the teachers concerned and the JMB supplies both students' individual record cards and a summary card for each school. The summary card provides space for teachers to indicate those areas of practical work which have been used in the assessment of the five qualities. The return to teachers for all the work involved lies in the beneficial effects that the planning of such assessment programmes can have upon teaching practice and course design.

It is perfectly possible to record performance in relation to the practical component of an internally or externally assessed course of study without making any specific judgment about that performance or taking it into consideration when making a final judgment. In such circumstances practical performance may either be simply described or used as a basis for admission to the examination itself. This occurs in the New Zealand Music examination referred to earlier. Here a practical record card is completed by the school at the end of the fourth and fifth form years. This contains details of instruments learnt, a description of the levels reached in instrumental playing backed up by any specialist external examination results. Similar information is provided about group activities such as choral singing and the teacher then gives an overall assessment on an A to E scale separately for Ability and Effort. Additionally just prior to the examination itself the school certifies for each pupil that a satisfactory level in practical music-making has been reached. Without this the pupil cannot sit for the written examination and hence cannot receive a certificate.

Project work

A project is in effect a large-scale set exercise from which time constraints have been largely removed. A very wide range of work is covered by the term 'project' and it can involve activities such as:

(a) Collecting data and analysing it;
(b) Engaging in open ended experiments in a laboratory;
(c) Making objects complete in themselves or as a part of larger studies;
(d) Identifying and endeavouring to solve problems;
(e) Investigating underlying concepts or principles.

These kinds of activities may be carried out by individuals or by groups. The assessment of project work raises issues similar to those raised by other forms of assessment but it does raise certain of them in rather stark terms and it is upon these that attention will be concentrated in this section. They are as follows:

1 Process versus product;
2 The role of the teacher;
3 The use of resources.

1   Most project work has in the past emphasised the finished product at the expense of the processes that have gone into achieving that product. The balance can be restored assuming it is considered desirable to do so in three main ways. First, by ensuring that the criteria used for assessing project work contain a proper emphasis upon process and that this is reflected in the judgments made about the work. Planning and the search for evidence, for example, would need greater weight than presentation in a History project. Second, by decreasing the emphasis upon a single big project and making instead more use of a series of mini-projects and third, by giving greater consideration to assessment in more than one dimension. In many projects it is inevitable that much if not all of the work will be derivative. History is a notable example of this although it is a valid comment for most subjects. What is important is not whether the work has been derived but whether it has been understood. Investigation of this point can only be undertaken if assessment takes place in more than one dimension. This means in effect a considerable extension of oral assessment since, as has already been suggested, the most useful way to explore understanding of work described in writing or undertaken in practical terms is to talk about it. Unfortunately the conduct of orals as has also been indicated earlier is demanding in both time and effort. Hence its extended use will need to be justified in terms of its educational value relative to other activities. There is no doubt however in the authors' minds that a lopsided picture is presented of many pupils as a result of single dimensional

assessment. Nowhere is this more true than with project work.

2 Project work draws particular attention to two important inter-connected issues which have significance for assessment as a whole. The first concerns the role of the teacher and the second the impact of factors outside the school. Teachers have tended to take two rather extreme views of their role in relation to project work. They have either provided the pupils with no help at all or they have treated it as a largely teacher dominated exercise. Neither of these has been particularly productive and what is wanted as so often in education is the middle way in which the teacher acts as an important resource while encouraging pupils to work on their own as much as possible.

It is of course impossible, even if it were thought desirable, to eliminate the influence of the home environment in the context of school performance. Project work, however, raises this issue in a particularly acute form. One is, moreover, continually having to consider work in which the degree of effort is not and cannot be reflected in the finished product and hence is often inadequately rewarded. A great deal can be done, as has already been said, to ensure that the criteria used for assessment reflect more than just surface polish and a great deal can also be done to improve the availability of resources. In the last resort, however, this situation shows up two of the major failings of our external examination system, failings which have been carried over into too many internal school assessment programmes. First there is the built-in assumption that all pupils start the race at the same time under the same general conditions. We assume therefore that all we need to do is to observe and classify their relative standing at the finishing post. Second, the system fails to take adequate account of qualities such as effort and persistence and they are in consequence rarely reflected in the awards made to pupils.

3 It would be fair to say that good project work rarely emerges from an environment which has inadequate resources. While such resources will and indeed must inevitably be wide-ranging both in human terms and in terms of material, the schools' and the teachers' concern will be centred on their

development, availability and methods of use. Many schools now recognise the importance of resources in the curriculum by establishing resource centres or resource banks and by employing qualified staff to run them. The essence of a good resource centre lies in its contents and in the ready availability of these contents to those who wish to use them. Its stock must result from the collaborate activity of many people, both teachers and taught, who in a very real sense make the resource centre a living and breathing thing. Resources must, above all, be flexible; books, while important, can be inflexible since they usually follow a predetermined pattern and answer as well as ask questions. Resources should provide the raw material which students and teachers can use to pose problems and then try to answer them on their own. The materials are in consequence infinitely variable in their origins and infintely variable in their 'ephemerality'. All good resource centres should contain a permanent hard core of reference material, a middle range of material which is maintained over a lengthy period but which is subject to frequent review and a substantial fluctuating body of material which comes and goes according to needs. One problem that often arises in relation to resource material, particularly in subjects like History where much of it is from another era, is the extent to which it should be adapted for present day use. This is an issue upon which teachers will have to make up their own minds. It would seem far better, however, that material should be used at the expense of an occasional 'anachronism' or over-simplification than that it should be unused in the interests of disciplinary purity.

Resource material does not, of course, consist solely of written material: pictures, models, components for models, theatre props, records, tapes, films and photographs all have their place and their value.

As with so much that is concerned with project work, the provision of adequate resources does not result from in-activity. It requires organisation, hard work and often careful structuring to ensure that resources are to be effectively used. In this as in so many other respects the role of the teacher is crucial.

The assessment of attitudes

Much greater attention has been paid in recent years within the secondary curriculum to what are frequently called attitudes. This is reflecting in practice the intent of the curriculum makers whose major emphasis in their general aims is usually placed upon non-cognitive outcomes. There has, however, been considerable confusion in the use of the word 'attitude' particularly in relation to assessment. Two meanings have indeed been attached to it although the distinction in practice is not as great as the account which follows would suggest. It has been used first as the psychologist would use it to indicate a person's disposition to respond to an educational or social situation in a particular manner. Such a disposition can be predictable and may well become relatively stable and enduring as a person matures. Attitudes in this sense are of considerable importance in the teaching/learning process and many indeed would regard the inculcating of appropriate attitudes in pupils as one of the main functions of education and in particular of a school system. The word attitude has also been used when referring to attributes of character and personality, which help pupils in their studies. As such they clearly fall outside Bloom's cognitive domain. It is this second use which is more immediately relevant to the debate currently taking place about the assessment of attitudes within the secondary curriculum, a debate largely sparked off by developments in Science and the Humanities.

The assessment of attitudes arouses great heat because it raises not only issues of practicality but also those of propriety. Even if we can assess in this area, say many teachers, we ought not to do so and in particular we ought never to use the results of such assessment as part of the evidence presented by public examinations. It is precisely this last issue that the recent curriculum projects in Science and the Humanities have raised. On the other hand if we do not assess in this area how can we justify in practice curriculum aims such as 'to develop an imaginative sympathy with subjective human experience'. This is typical of the generalised and largely meaningless aims which curriculum makers tend to use particularly by way of introduction to their proposals. Ought we not either to scrap such aims or attempt to substantiate them? In the last resort, of course, the decision as to whether or not to attempt to assess attitudes is a personal one but it is also one to which it is easier to say 'no' if the techniques for assessment are unfamiliar. Here as elsewhere in assessment the question of what we ought to assess precedes that of how are we going to do it. Definition is thus a necessary, albeit a difficult, preliminary to consideration of methods. Classifications systems of the kind developed for the cognitive domain may provide a useful stimulus to systematic thought here also. The Krathwohl taxonomy for example uses the degree to which a person accepts and adopts an educational experience (internalises) as the underlying principle upon which to classify. Five levels of acceptance are proposed:

1 Receiving/Attending;
2 Responding;
3 Valuing;
4 Organisation of Values;
5 Characterisation.

In other words the stages move from simply receiving an educational experience to the complete acceptance of a way of life. This could be applied for example to the kind of aim that is often found in a science curriculum, namely 'to develop a concern for the environment'. The lowest possible level of responding is that individuals should be aware that there is such a thing as the environment and that they are a part of it. This is worth very little on its own and strictly speaking an attitude cannot be said to have been adopted until the person concerned has internalised the experience to at least the level of responding: for example, 'has shown an interest in his/her own role within the environment'. This kind of expansion of the original aim can be undertaken for all five stages of the taxonomy as it can for other similar general aims such as 'to encourage the growth of aesthetic sensitivity (from the New Zealand Music syllabus), 'to develop an appreciation for literature' and 'to show sensitivity towards other people'. Many teachers find it neither easy nor very helpful particularly for assessment purposes to classify attitudes in this way. Of more immediate use, especially in the classroom, is the development of scales in relation to which an individual's opinion can be recorded or alongside which individuals can be placed in terms of their characteristics. The resulting information can be quantified and used for a variety of purposes. The use of scales is indeed the basis of attitude assessment. Like abilities, attitudes may be regarded as existing in different amounts rather than as being simply present or absent. Most attitudes are indeed bi-polar, varying from a maximum in one direction through a mid-point to a maximum in another direction. In our assessment of cognitive abilities particularly in public examinations we tend not to concern ourselves with this bi-polarity but start instead at the mid-point to which we usually affix the label zero and go in only one direction.

The two most common methods of constructing scales to measure attitudes in the sense in which the word was first used in this section are called Thurstone- and Likert-type scales respectively. Both methods depend upon people signifying their agreement or disagreement with a series of statements about the object or concept towards which their attitude is being assessed. In a Thurstone type scale those responding to it have to go through a set of selected statements and agree or disagree with each one of them in turn, for example, 'Comprehensive Education has led to a fall in reading standards.' The decision as to whether or not to include a particular statement in the scale results from the rating of a wide variety of statements by a number of experienced judges. As a result a scale value is attached to each statement and it is this which determines its inclusion or exclusion. In a Likert type scale no such preliminary judgment takes place and the respondents are asked to indicate the extent of their agreement or disagreement to each statement. For this purpose a five point scale is normally used: Strongly Agree, Agree, Undecided, Strongly Disagree, Disagree. The construction of such scales is almost certainly best left to those who specialise in this area although it is very useful for teachers to know how they are constructed in order that they can use them with understanding. Scales can, however, be directly useful in classroom and in external assessment. As has already been indicated, recent Science curricula have emphasised the importance of such non-cognitive attributes as persistence and enthusiasm (the second use of the word attitude). It would be possible to devise three or even five point scales to identify degrees of persistence or enthusiasm as for example, 'very persistent', 'persistent', 'totally lacking in persistence' and to assess pupils either periodically or on one single occasion against such scales. Such assessment flounders, however, upon the vagueness of words or phrases such as 'very' or 'totally lacking' and the resulting problem of achieving any kind of consistent judgment. More helpful is the approach already suggested in relation to the assessment of practical skills: namely the listing of attitudes of a persistent pupil or one lacking in persistence in terms of the relevant subject and then combining the resulting descriptions into a scale. For example:

Persistence:
1 Most persistent and thorough, will see a task through even if it is rather distasteful. Checks and cross-checks his work without prompting.
2 More than usually persistent — works hard without constant supervision. Can be left to get on with it, is not put off by minor upsets or snags.
3 Not outstanding in any way — gets on with what he is clearly expected or told to do, but does not show undue patience, application or thoroughness.
4 Rather easily put off and distracted. Soon grows tired of a piece of work, needs constant jogging and supervision.
5 Very lacking indeed in concentration and persistence. Needs to be watched all the time. Finds it very hard to complete a task.

The bi-polarity of such a scale stands out clearly. Such scales have been successfully constructed by teachers and applied in public examinations in Science as well as in a wide variety of internal assessment. While it would be quite wrong to suggest that the use of scales such as these for assessing attitudes will provide easy solutions to the problems involved, it does suggest that it is realistic to look for a greater degree of precision in this area in future. Their development also suggests that those using them will need to develop skills in observation to which they may not previously have given much attention. It goes without saying that success here as in any other educational activity emerges not by chance but as a result of well thought out instructions, careful planning and considerable practice.

Chapter four

Making use of the results of assessment

In order to make use of the information provided by assessment its results need to be described in ways which are both convenient and meaningful. There are a variety of ways in which this can be done for example, marks, percentages and letter grades. Of these the classroom teacher is most likely to use marks. Marks are certainly convenient but are they meaningful? Let us look at a situation which happens frequently. Young John gets home from school and announces proudly to Dad, 'I got 14 out of 20 for my history test today.' More often than not Dad's reaction will be along the following lines, 'Well done lad, here's 5p, keep up the good work.' He might even add, 'That's better than I ever did at History when I was at school.' If on the other hand Mum asks Jane how she got on in her French test and Jane rather glumly says, 'I got 5 out of 20', Mum will almost inevitably say something about the need for harder work.

The reactions of John's and Jane's parents could, of course, have been different. They might have asked any or all of the following questions: 'How many others in the class scored 14 (or 5)?' or 'What was the average mark in the class for the test?' or 'What position did you come in class in the test?' or 'How many marks did you get on your last History (or French) test?' They might even have asked what the test was for. The children also could have added to their original statements. Jane in particular might have tried to justify herself by saying that it was a stupid test because it did not ask about any of the things they had done in class or she might have said that Miss Smith never gave high marks in tests.

Making use of the results of assessment

All Mum's and Dad's possible or actual questions and Jane's excuses draw attention in different ways to the fundamental point that a test score whether it takes the form of a mark or a percentage or a grade has no meaning on its own. It acquires meaning only when it is considered alongside other information. As soon as a variety of information is involved then presentation becomes important. If information, whatever its nature, is to be put to use then it must be presented in ways which can be readily understood by those likely to refer to it. Indeed, the requirements of the user will to an extent condition the form of presentation. What satisfies the needs, for example, of the teacher in the classroom may well not satisfy the needs of the employer. For everyone, however, the two principles of never viewing test scores in isolation and of always presenting information about them clearly and simply remain cardinal.

Let us apply these two principles to John's mark in the History test, 14 out of 20. In order to satisfy the first we need to know the marks obtained by all John's classmates in the History test in which John gained 14. (We may in addition need to know the marks obtained by the class in other History tests but that point will be returned to later.) These marks might have been 1, 15, 5, 7, 12, 3, 14, 14, 8, 2, 19, 5, 18, 6, 13, 7, 17, 7, 13 and 14. From this rather jumbled set of figures (to be more precise we should say that they are put down in random order) a great deal of information can be extracted relatively quickly, particularly when the number and size of the marks is relatively small as it will be for most class groups. We can tell, for example, that twenty people took this particular test (not, incidentally, that there are twenty people in John's class), that two people in addition to John obtained 14 marks, that four people scored more than 14 and thirteen people scored less than 14 and that the highest mark was 19 and the lowest mark was 1. All this information relates, of course, to this particular test only. Its provision and the ability to assimilate it quickly would be helped if the marks were presented rather more systematically. The first thing that could be done would be to arrange them in ascending or descending order, namely:

1, 2, 3, 5, 5, 6, 7, 7, 7, 8, 12, 13, 13,

14, 14, 14, 15, 17, 18, 19

This presentation highlights some points which did not stand out so clearly when the marks were in random order, namely that the marks (out of 20) are very widely dispersed and that the test has divided the class into two equal groups: those who obtained marks between 1 and 8 (ten in all) and those who obtained marks between 12 and 19 (ten in all). Nobody obtained a mark of between 9 and 11. By listing the pupils' names with their marks a rank order can be produced for the test. This more orderly presentation also aids the calculation of two useful measures called the Range and the Mean. The Range for any group of numbers (in this case test marks) indicates the extent to which they are dispersed and is found by subtracting the lowest mark obtained from the highest mark obtained. In this test this is 19–1 and the range therefore is 18. This incidentally is very high, the maximum possible for the test being 20–0 or 20. The Mean or average mark for the test is found by dividing the total number of marks obtained by the number who took the test. In this case $\frac{200}{20}$ or 10. It should be noted that the mean as here can be a mark obtained by no-one who actually took the test. It will, moreover, frequently not be a whole number. The Mean should not be confused with the Median which is the mark obtained by the pupil at the mid-point in the rank order. When an even number of pupils are involved, as in the case of John's class, the Median is the average of the marks obtained by the two in the middle, i.e. the tenth and eleventh pupil who in this case obtained 8 and 12 respectively. The Median is, therefore, 10. It happens on this occasion that the Mean and the Median are both 10 but this need not necessarily be the case.

Before leaving the presentation of information two further

methods will be considered. One piece of information which does not stand out very clearly from looking at a list of marks, particularly if they are large in size or number, is the frequency with which each mark is used. This point can be shown much more clearly by a cumulative frequency chart or table, as shown in Table 1.

TABLE 1

Mark	Frequency of occurrence in test	Cumulative frequency
0	0	0
1	1	1
2	1	2
3	1	3
4	0	3
5	2	5
6	1	6
7	3	9
8	1	10
9	0	10
10	0	10
11	0	10
12	1	11
13	2	13
14	3	16
15	1	17
16	0	17
17	1	18
18	1	19
19	1	20
20	0	20

For those who prefer a visual presentation (and this probably includes a majority of teachers) this information can be presented in the form of a histogram (opposite).

The absence of marks in the middle, of course, gives this particular histogram a rather odd appearance. In practice a histogram will be the more useful of the two methods for classroom teachers concerned with relatively small numbers. A cumulative frequency table is likely to be more useful with larger numbers. In such circumstances it would almost certainly not show the frequency of occurrence for each individual mark but would instead show the frequency of occurrence within groups of marks, for example 0—4, 5—9, 10—14 or 0—9, 10—19 and so on.

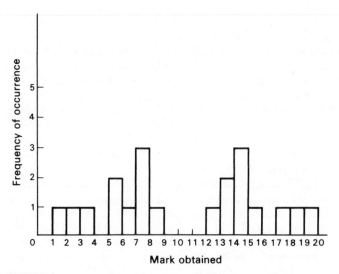

FIGURE 3

The reader, it is hoped, will by now have appreciated that the form of presentation can be affected by the nature of the questions that are to be asked of the information. This is very different, however, from the presentation determining the questions that can be asked, although in practice the dividing line between the two may be a very narrow one. Those who use information must, therefore, always be on their guard against asking only those questions whose answers seem readily obtainable. Asking the right questions is more important than providing acceptable answers to the wrong ones.

What use is all this information, whose extraction and assembly incidentally has required no more than the ability to add, subtract, multiply and divide? In order to answer this let us relate our information to the questions which Mum and Dad could have asked about John's mark of 14 out of 20. We now know that two other classmates also obtained 14 marks (frequency) that the average mark for the test was 10 (the mean), John's mark thus being 4 above the mean. We also know that John was fifth in the class in this test (his position in the rank order). We still cannot answer the last specific question, 'How many marks did John obtain in his last history test?' nor have we yet considered the general question of what the history test was for or the relevance or otherwise of Jane's excuses. To these we will return later. What we have done is to provide John's parents with far more useful information about John's performance than they could have obtained from his original statement, 'I got 14 out of 20.' There seems as a result to be rather more justification than there was for Dad's original comment.

John's parents are not, however, the only people to whom such information might be useful, there is John's teacher and John himself. Let us look, therefore, at what John's teacher can find out from the information so far obtained about the history test which it is assumed that he or she set. It is a test — on the evidence be it noted of the people who took it — which

1 spread out the marks very widely indeed (the range);
2 proved difficult (indeed very difficult for some students and easy (indeed very easy) for others (cumulative frequency);
3 had an average mark of exactly half the total (the mean).

The sources of information for these statements, as with the earlier remarks about John's performance, are given in brackets. The crucial question that the teacher now has to answer is, 'Did I intend all these things to happen?' If the answer is 'No' then the supplementary question 'Why did they happen?' ought to be asked and answered.

These questions cannot be answered without going back to the purposes of the assessment and the objectives being tested and hence without going back to the pupils, the schools and the subjects involved. For the classroom teacher this is possible; for an examining agency operating on a large scale such as a GCE or CSE Board it is much more difficult. The objectives of its examinations, indeed its view of a particular subject, must inevitably be a generalised view of what its advisers at the time consider to be significant. This in its turn will generalise the value of any information that may be made available from its examinations.

Teachers can thus use information from their own assessment for improving instruction and diagnosing the strengths and weaknesses of individual pupils while the examining board's primary use will be to improve the quality of the examination itself. Within this general distinction, however, teachers and agencies are likely to use the information they obtain in a variety of different ways. For example, the data about the history test taken by John ought to produce a very different response from a teacher who had set it prior to covering the topic in class with a view to using its results to plan instruction than from one who had set it as a mastery test after instruction. Similarly the response to the data by a GCE Board which had intended the test to discriminate at the top and bottom ends of the ability range of those taking it ought to take a different form from that of a board which had intended it to spread candidates evenly over the available mark range.

All this, of course, suggests that the question 'What was the test for?' is a very perceptive one in relation to any evaluation of a single mark like John's 14. Different purposes could make it a satisfactory or an unsatisfactory mark. This is also true of Jane's 5 in French although she clearly thought it to be a bad mark and assumed that her parents would do the same. The irony is that the excuses she uses — tests designed to reveal weaknesses and severity of marking — could both form part of a well-designed and deliberately planned instructional assessment programme. Regrettably, they could equally well be the result of arbitrary action by the teacher although it is interesting that Jane does not suggest that Miss Smith's marking is inconsistent or unreliable.

This chapter has so far concentrated upon information that

can be obtained from a single mark in a single test when it is considered alongside other marks from the same test. Any systematically designed programme of instruction and assessment will however collect information from a variety of sources. Of these the results of tests are likely to be one of the most important. Such programmes may, moreover, culminate in external examinations whose results will form a major source of information for users outside the school. This raises a new problem, that of accumulating information about individuals or groups in such a way that comparisons can fairly be made. In such circumstances presentation has to concern itself with developing methods which will draw attention to the various facets of individual character and performance that can emerge from complete programmes.

Most teachers deal with the problem of accumulating information with disarming simplicity; they simply add together the marks obtained from tests and arrive at a total mark or grade. This determines the end of term or end of year order of merit and this in its turn all too often forms the basis of the pupil's termly or annual report. Schools on occasion go even further and award prizes on the basis of adding together marks obtained by pupils from different subjects. The person with the most marks gets the prize. Is either of these actions justified? The answer is 'No, definitely not', for the simple reason that like is not being added to like.

It is not perhaps too difficult to appreciate that two marks of 10/20 obtained by the same pupil in tests in Mathematics and English are not necessarily the same. There are many reasons for this, some of which have already been mentioned: the purposes of the two tests and the objectives being tested may have been quite different. They may have contained different types of questions or used different techniques of assessment, they will almost certainly have been marked by different people and could have been taken by the pupils on different days. It is, however, less easy to appreciate that all these same factors can apply when the pupil's two marks of 10/20 come from two tests in the same subject. Thus marks, whether they are obtained from different tests in the same subjects or from tests in different subjects, should never be added together until they have been put upon a common scale or have been 'standardised' to use the technical term. This ought also to be done when the different tests form the component parts of a public examination designed to test different skills, say a project, an objective test and essay questions in a GCE or CSE History examination, although in practice this rarely happens.

It needs also to be emphasised that no score or mark has any absolute value. It is simply the score obtained by a particular person in a particular test on a particular day. On another day the same person taking the same test could obtain a different score. There are many reasons for this, some obvious, some less obvious. The concept of error of measurement to which this draws attention is, however, a very complex one and will not be covered in this book. It is sufficient here to appreciate that the problem exists.

The alternative to standardisation is to accept that the marks are different and adopt presentations which emphasise this. Methods of description which draw attention to a variety of facets are often given the name profiles. It is with standardisation and profiles that much of the rest of this chapter will be concerned.

Standardisation of marks

When two or more sets of marks are considered alongside each other the two principal features which distinguish them are their means (the average mark) and the extent to which the marks are spread around the mean. In a normal distribution one would expect this spread to follow a consistent pattern as Figure 4 (p. 100) shows.

One can define a normal distribution in a variety of rather complex ways but put in very simple terms it means that in any randomly selected sample of reasonable size the trait being looked at (in this case the marks obtained by pupils in tests) is distributed symmetrically about the mean and can be

Making use of the results of assessment

illustrated by a bell shaped curve. As Figure 4 shows, the largest number of marks or pupils or whatever, is to be found at the peak or fattest part of the curve.

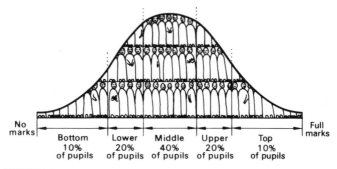

FIGURE 4

The more important of the two distinguishing features and therefore the one which will exercise the greatest influence in any combination of sets of scores is the spread of the marks about the mean. This was noted earlier in Chapter 1 in the discussion upon weighting with reference to a four-part assessment in English. When considering the spread of marks within any test it is not sufficient to look at the upper and lower limits only, and hence the range; the spread of the intermediate marks must also be looked at. This is because a single exceptionally high or exceptionally low mark could make the range for the test appear high whereas in reality the overwhelming majority of the marks were bunched in the middle. An amusing illustration of this occurs in a very worthwhile book on statistics called *Fred Learns Basic Statistics*, details of which are given in the reading for this chapter. A survey of lectures at a university shows that the ages of those attending were 18, 21, 19, 19, 20, 18, 54, 20, 19. The range is thus 36 (54—18). Yet if the student aged 54 is eliminated (was the lecturer added by mistake or was there a mature student?) the range becomes 3 (21—18). In such circumstances the range is clearly misleading. What is required is a measure of dispersion or spread which takes account of such 'freaks'. This is

100

provided by the standard deviation for which the symbol is σ. This is calculated according to a formula which takes into account how far each mark in the set is from the mean. For the mathematically inclined the formula is

$$\sigma = \sqrt{\frac{\Sigma(X - M)^2}{N}}$$

where X is any mark, M is the mean of all marks, N is the number of marks, Σ is the capital letter sigma in the Greek alphabet and denotes summation i.e. ΣX is the sum of all Xs. A worked example using John's history test may help the reader to understand the calculation (see Table 2).

There is, however, no need to go through this process every time you wish to work out a standard deviation. One of two alternatives could be adopted. One is a 'short-cut' calculation which can be readily undertaken, the other is to accept the formula and simply make use of the calculated standard deviation without attempting to work it out. A useful short-cut calculation originally devised by W. L. Jenkins of Lehigh University, USA, which appears in *Short-Cut Statistics for the Teacher* by Paul Diederich of Educational Testing Service, Princeton, USA, has for its formula

$$\frac{\sigma}{(SD)} = \frac{\text{Sum of high sixth of test scores} - \text{sum of low sixth of test scores}}{\text{Half the number of pupils taking the particular test}}$$

Taking John's history test once again this formula would work out as follows:

Number of pupils = 20   One sixth = $3\frac{1}{3}$
Sum of high sixth of test scores = 19, 18, 17 + 5 ($\frac{1}{3}$ of 15) = 59
Sum of low sixth of test scores = 1, 2, 3 + 1.66 ($\frac{1}{3}$ of 5) = 7.66
Half the number of pupils = 10
Therefore SD = $\dfrac{59 - 7.66}{10}$

$= \dfrac{51.34}{10}$

$= 5.13$

Making use of the results of assessment

This varies very slightly from the 5.38 derived from the full formula but illustrates the point that most short-cut methods lose their accuracy as the sample becomes smaller and less normal. This, of course, can easily happen with the relatively small numbers that teachers have in their classes.

TABLE 2

Marks obtained	Deviations less mean	Squared deviations
X	(X − M)	(X − M)²
1	−9	81
2	−8	64
3	−7	49
5	−5	25
5	−5	25
6	−4	16
7	−3	9
7	−3	9
7	−3	9
8	−2	4
12	2	4
13	3	9
13	3	9
14	4	16
14	4	16
14	4	16
15	5	25
17	7	49
18	8	64
19	9	81
200		580

Mean (M) = 10 $\Sigma (X - M)^2 = 580$ N = 20

Standard deviation $= \sqrt{\dfrac{\Sigma(X - M)^2}{N}} = \sqrt{29} = 5.385$

Assuming that we can either calculate the standard deviation or are told what it is we now have the basis upon which we can standardise scores or marks to a common scale. A school situation which should require such standardisation to take place is one in which the end of term order of merit for a particular form with all its consequences is based upon a series of marks derived from different subjects (we are not incidentally concerned here with the question of how these marks were derived). In order to cut down the numbers involved a selection of five students will be chosen with their end of term marks in English and Mathematics (see Table 3). One would not, of course, normally use such a small sample.

TABLE 3

Pupil	English mark	Mathematics mark	Total
A	58	4	62
B	54	10	64
C	50	18	68
D	46	32	78
E	44	42	86

Assuming that the teachers concerned had not read this chapter and added the English and Mathematics marks together then the final rank order would be as in Table 4 with Pupil E first.

TABLE 4

Pupil	English rank order	Mathematics rank order	Final rank order
A	(1)	(5)	(5)
B	(2)	(4)	(4)
C	(3)	(3)	(3)
D	(4)	(2)	(2)
E	(5)	(1)	(1)

Let us now standardise the marks obtained in the two subjects. The effect upon the rank order will be significant since the narrow spread of the English marks as compared with the Mathematics marks meant that the latter subject dominated the final order of merit when the two sets of marks were simply added together.

Making use of the results of assessment

Standardisation is achieved by expressing the deviation of the marks from the mean mark in units of a standard deviation. In the example we are considering there are two means and standard deviations, one for the English marks (Mean 50.4 SD 5.12) and one for the Mathematics marks (Mean 21.2 SD 14.01). Either of these can be used as the basis for standardisation; alternatively, a completely new mean and standard deviation can be chosen to which both sets of scores are standardised. IQ tests, for example, are scaled to a mean of 100 and a standard deviation of 15. One which is commonly used, is a scale with a mean of 50 and a standard deviation of 15. The working out of the necessary calculations manually is a time-consuming process. We will, therefore, assume that they have been carried out and will show the effect upon both sets of marks and hence upon the rank order of standardising first the English scores to the Mathematics mean and standard deviation and second both English and Mathematics scores to a scale with a mean of 50 and a standard deviation of 15.

The means and standard deviations of the English and Mathematics marks as we already know are as in Table 5.

TABLE 5

	English	Mathematics
Mean	50.4	21.2
SD	5.12	14.01

By substituting the English marks in the following formula one is able to convert them to a set of marks with the same mean and standard deviation as the Mathematics marks:

$$\frac{E - 50.4}{5.12} = \frac{E_1 - 21.2}{14.01}$$

E is the original English mark

E_1 is the scaled (converted) English mark

In Table 6 the converted English marks are added to the original Mathematics marks to obtain a new set of total marks with a different order of merit.

TABLE 6

Converted English marks	Mathematics marks	Total marks	Position
42.0	4	46.0	1
31.1	10	41.1	4
20.1	18	38.1	5
9.2	32	41.2	3
3.7	42	45.7	2

If each set of marks were converted to a mark distribution with a mean of 50 and a standard deviation of 15, one would obtain the sets of marks in Table 7.

TABLE 7

Converted English mark	Converted Mathematics mark	Total marks	Position
72.3	31.6	103.9	1
60.5	38.0	98.5	4
48.8	46.6	95.4	5
37.1	61.6	98.7	3
31.3	72.3	103.6	2

It will be noted that the order of merit is the same in each case.

It is hoped that this illustration will demonstrate how essential it is to standardise marks derived from different sources if justice is to be done for all students across subjects.

There is, however, a much simpler method which can be used by the classroom teacher to standardise marks. To use this method it is necessary to know the mean and standard deviation of the original marks to be standardised and the mean and standard deviation to which the original marks are to be scaled. A considerable amount has been written in this chapter about the calculation of the standard deviation and for classroom use it is quite adequate to use the 'sixths' method which has been described earlier as a short-cut method for providing a useful approximate standard deviation.

This simpler method for standardising marks is a graphical

one and is best illustrated by an example, in this case the scaling of the English marks as given in Table 3 to the same mean and standard deviation as the Mathematics marks in the same Table. In other words a set of marks having a mean of 50.4 and a standard deviation of 5.1 is to be standardised to a mean of 21.2 and a standard deviation of 14.0. (The scale used in most graphs does not allow one to plot more than one decimal place, hence 5.12 becomes 5.1 and 14.01 becomes 14.0.)

The procedure is as follows:

1 Use one of the two axes of the graph for the English marks and the other for the Mathematics marks. It is helpful in labelling the axes to include in each case the values of the mean and the standard deviation.

2 Plot three points, A, B and C
   A — Opposite the English mean (50.4) and the Mathematics mean (21.2)
   B — Opposite the English mean plus one standard deviation (55.5) and the Mathematics mean plus one standard deviation (35.2)
      i.e. English: 50.4 plus 5.1 = 55.5
      Mathematics: 21.2 plus 14.0 = 35.2
   C — Opposite the English mean minus one standard deviation (45.3) and the Mathematics mean minus one standard deviation (7.2)
      i.e. English: 50.4 minus 5.1 = 45.3
      Mathematics: 21.2 minus 14.0 = 7.2

3 Join the points by a straight line.

You will then find that by reading vertically to the line you have plotted, it is possible to convert English scores with the original mean of 50.4 and standard deviation of 5.1 to a mean of 21.2 and standard deviation of 14.0. The illustration of the conversion of the original English mark of 58 is shown on the graph. You can use this graph to check the converted English marks in Table 6 which have been worked out using the formula.

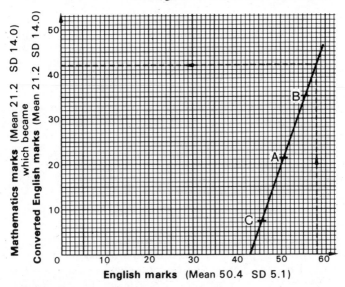

FIGURE 5

It must be emphasised that the scale of the graph makes some approximation necessary. It is unlikely to occur in practice that teachers would wish to work with other than whole marks.

The graph (Figure 5) can, of course, also be used to convert a set of marks having a mean of 21.2 and standard deviation of 14.0 to one with a mean of 50.4 and standard deviation of 5.1.

Often, however, it is, as has already been indicated, useful to convert sets of marks with different means and standard deviations to sets which have the same mean and standard deviation, for example a mean of 50 and a standard deviation of 15. From the example already given on the graph it is easy to see how this can be done. Use one axis for the set of marks to be scaled and the other axis to show marks with a mean of 50 and having a standard deviation of 15. The task is therefore exactly the same as that already illustrated in Figure 5, it is only the values that differ.

Making use of the results of assessment

The purpose of this section has been a two-fold one. First, to emphasise the vital importance of standardisation when using information acquired from a variety of sources for a single purpose such as awarding a form prize. Second, to provide the reader with some straightforward methods of undertaking the task of standardisation. The next section will be concerned with ways in which this same variety of information can be presented in order that it can be readily understood.

Profiles

The term profile in relation to educational assessment is used to describe multi-dimensional methods of presenting the results, however expressed, of the assessment of pupils and/or their work. A profile is not a method of assessment but a method of presentation and in consequence it is only as full and as varied as the information it seeks to present. Profiles, therefore, differ from each other in two major ways: in the content of what is presented and in the ways in which that content is presented. The presentation can, for example, be diagrammatic, graphical, tabular or verbal to name but four possibilities. The histogram which appeared earlier in this chapter is a simple profile presenting information as it does about the numbers of pupils obtaining particular marks upon a particular test. A reference on behalf of an applicant for a post is also a profile, this time a verbal one. Here the coverage is determined by the requirements of the employer asking for the reference as modified by the person supplying it.

In general verbal profiles like school reports or references tend to provide a greater range of information than do visual profiles. This greater range makes it possible to build up a more rounded picture of the person or attribute being described. Visual profiles contain less information for the simple reason that they have to present it simultaneously to the viewer and not a piece at a time as occurs when reading is involved. For this reason visual presentations are more frequently concerned with information about the performance of individuals than about the individuals themselves. The very wide variety of possible profiles cannot possibly be covered in this short section. Instead two illustrations will be given both of which aim to provide information which will be helpful to pupils and teachers. The second unlike the first is also concerned with helping the potential employer.

The earlier chapters in this book have drawn attention to the importance of stating objectives for courses of instruction and their related assessment. This has increasingly become a feature of both classroom practice and public examinations. Much of the value of doing this in terms of feedback will, however, be lost if information is not reported in relation to these stated objectives whatever they may be. This has implications for course presentation, assessment and the reporting of performance. With well presented objectives which are successfully worked out in the classroom through appropriate teaching strategies and assessment, the basis is provided for a variety of approaches to presenting information about selected aspects of individual or class performance. Take for example the proposal for a CSE Mode 3 in English as shown on pp. 110–11.

In the complete proposal there are further sections on Literature and the Mass Media and additional columns in each section which provide more detail about the assessment procedures and about methods of moderation. A great deal of information will become available from the assessment of such courses. The problem is how best to report it. Individual student or class performance could, for example, be reported in relation to the methods of assessment as shown in Figure 6 on p. 112.

The data shown in Figure 6 indicates that for the stated period, this could be a month or a term or a year, the pupil in question has obtained 40 marks out of 100 on his unseen examination, 70 marks out of 100 on his course work and 50 marks out of 100 on his periodic class tests. Different scales and different methods of assessment could, of course, be chosen.

CSE Mode 3 in English

ORAL

Objectives	Assessed by	Criteria for assessment	Weighting
A. To teach listening skills through: Aural comprehension	Periodic assessment	Understanding the meaning of the passage. No mechanical skills to be assessed	12% (3 × 4%) each passage to be weighted 4%
B. To teach direct communicative skills by: (i) Use of the telephone (ii) Interviews (iii) Discussions	Continuous assessment	1. Ability to give and understand clear messages 2. Ability to maintain communicative relationship 3. Ability to present an argument coherently	8%
C. To teach awareness of the suitability of different forms of speech through knowledge of: (i) different registers (ii) difference between verbal and non-verbal communication (iii) skills of reading for entertainment	Continuous assessment	1. Ability to recognise the appropriateness of different registers, and the presence of non-verbal communication 2. Ability to read interestingly	5%

ENGLISH SKILLS

Objectives	Assessed by	Criteria for Assessment	Weighting
A. To develop comprehension skills	Written examination	Being able to answer questions which will be set on a passage or passages to test any or all of the following skills: (i) the ability to select, arrange and express in own words the information from passage(s); (ii) the ability to interpret details from the passage(s); (iii) the ability to understand particular words and images used by the author (in this case no question will ask the candidate to define single words or phrases); (iv) the ability to apply ideas in the passage(s) to other contexts; (v) the ability to comment knowledgeably upon the form and kind of approach used by the author.	10%
B. To develop ability in utilitarian English in any *one* of the following: (i) a letter appropriate in every way to a situation (ii) instructions in continuous prose or tabulated layout (iii) a factual record of events	Written examination	1. Accuracy in all uses of English 2. Awareness of the appropriateness of various forms of written English 3. Ability to arrange information in a logical sequence	5%
PERSONAL WRITING			
To develop an awareness of the creative powers of the English Language	Course work	Evidence of sincerity, freshness of vision and expression and an appreciation of the dynamic nature of language	15%

Making use of the results of assessment

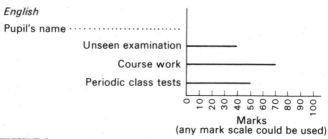

FIGURE 6

If as occurs here the performance upon each of the chosen dimensions, in this case forms of assessment, is reported upon a common scale then standardisation must take place before the reporting occurs. If this does not happen then comparisons cannot be made.

Alternatively the reporting could be based upon the achievement of the stated objectives. One way of presenting such information in relation say to the oral for a whole class or a single pupil or all boys, to name three possibilities, would be as in Figure 7.

A, B, C, D are the stated objectives taken from the oral section of the course. A could be Aural Comprehension, B Communication Skills, C Knowledge of Different Registers, D Reading Skills. The numbers 1, 2, 3, 4, 5 constitute a rating scale which has the following labels attached to it. 1 − Very bad; 2 − Poor; 3 − Reasonable; 4 − Good; 5 − Very good.

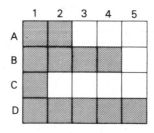

FIGURE 7

The data given in the illustration when related to an individual pupil would state, relative to the group as a whole, that he or she was poor at Aural Comprehension, had good Communication Skills, was very bad at Knowledge of Different Registers and had very good Reading Skills. It will be noted that the skills themselves are fairly generalised. With the exception perhaps of C they could all be broken down in much greater detail. The reader can readily work out from the English proposals different methods of presentation and different dimensions upon which to report. The data can be systematically stored and kept up-to-date and a mine of information will result for teachers to monitor their own performances and those of their pupils. The data can also be used to supply information for public examinations which make use as many now do of internal and/or continuously assessed elements to supplement terminal written tests. The tragedy is that the results of these public examinations are currently reported in terms of a single overall grade A, B, C or 1, 2, 3 etc. Such grades provide little or nothing in the way of feedback for the teacher and the pupil and until more helpful methods are adopted the value and hence the use of such examinations for evaluation and diagnosis will remain severely restricted. Initially, new methods need not be elaborate or sophisticated. A start could be made, for example, by reporting oral and written performance in Modern Languages separately and providing two grades instead of one. This would be immediately helpful to both teacher and employer and might stimulate demands for further information.

Another form of profile is exemplified by the Swindon Record of Personal Achievement (RPA) Scheme. This, as the reader will realise, has close links with school reports and references, although the RPA is far more elaborate and its purposes are significantly different from either of these.

The basic aim of the RPA which was introduced originally for all secondary school pupils in the county borough of Swindon between the ages of 14 and 16 is as follows:

1 To develop personal qualities that have value in family life, citizenship, leisure and work.

113

Making use of the results of assessment

It hopes to achieve this by

2 encouraging pupils to discover and develop their strengths
   for their own satisfaction and the benefit of others;
3 encouraging pupils to recognise their weaknessess and to
   learn how to minimise their importance and influence;
4 enabling pupils to learn about the world of work, about
   the community, about leisure opportunities, so that they
   can make the best of their best qualities.

The methods used to achieve these aims are

1 To provide an immediate and continuous record of all
   successful achievements inside and outside school, stored
   in a four part folder which will become the property of
   the pupil on leaving school;
2 To allow the pupil to decide what constitutes an achievement;
3 To ask a responsible adult to check and sign for the
   accuracy of each item;
4 To include in the record only facts accurately stated and
   adequately described and to exclude comparisons
   between pupils and assessments relating to other work;
5 To encourage all those who are concerned in the
   education of each student to help to record achievements on cards that have been designed to suit:
      group and individual projects, courses, lectures, visits,
      service to others, following instructions, timekeeping,
      assignments, creative work, reading, craft work, oral
      work, individual physical performances, team playing,
      leisure interests and pursuits, expeditions, residential
      courses;
6 To leave the schools free to determine and adapt the
   curriculum according to immediate and developing
   needs.

The record is not intended to compete with public
examinations but to supplement the information these can

114

give with different information differently presented. The RPA may, however, if the pupil wishes it contain examination results. It is not a school report since its content is chosen by the pupils themselves and its role here as with public examinations is intended to be a complementary one.

This brief reference to some contrasting profiles will, it is hoped, have further underlined the value of information which has been carefully collected through a mixture of formal and informal assessment and presented in ways which will facilitate its use. This applies equally to information which has been collected for a specific purpose and to that which has been collected in order to provide a comprehensive picture of an individual, a course of study or an institution.

Quality control

In considering standardisation and profiles, the assumption has been made that the assessment which has produced the marks or which has been described has been of good quality. Its quality will, of course, depend upon the expertise of those who have constructed it and the extent to which those concerned have been successful in relating the assessment to purpose and objectives, to pupil, to subject and to school. Although, as this book has been at pains to point out, assessment is an activity in which all teachers are bound to engage as an integral part of their classroom activity, it would be a mistake to assume that all are equally proficient at it. Proficiency can, of course, be improved by practice and by collaboration with colleagues but it can also be improved even for the most accomplished, particularly where written questions are concerned, by criticism based upon information obtained from systematic analysis. Those questions which survive this process can be stored or banked. A system of quality control can thus be developed involving the three stages of pre-testing, analysis and banking. The first has already been referred to in Chapter 2 and the other two will be the subject of this section. Classroom teachers may well regard what has just been said and what will follow, although the description will be a relatively brief one, as being both irrelevant to their needs and out of the question in terms of the time and resources necessary for its accomplishment. Nothing could be further from the truth. Any teacher worth his salt carries out these three stages when preparing, for example, an end of term written test. The way in which they are carried out is, however, more often than not, very informal. It consists of having used certain questions over the years (pre-testing) whose degree of difficulty and ability to spread out pupils (analysis) have been recorded in the teacher's mind (banking). Some teachers are more systematic than this in the sense that they maintain records of question use, store past tests and write comments alongside the stored questions. There is, however, a vast gulf in this area between most of what goes on in the classroom and the kind of programme which a large public examining board will undertake, although there is a good case for suggesting that teachers in a school or group of schools could co-operate with advantage to narrow this gap. The informality of much of what occurs in the classroom is further accentuated by the fact that pre-testing, analysis and banking are best suited to dealing with written questions which can be marked either right or wrong whereas a great deal of classroom assessment is not of this kind, and involves continuous writing and oral and practical work. Despite this the principles underlying the three activities are important and their acceptance would benefit classroom practice. The principle underlying both pre-testing and analysis is that we ought to know as much as possible about how any assessment will work before using it in a real situation, e.g. if we wish to set a difficult written question or a demanding oral test we ought to do so by design and not by accident. The saying 'Ask a stupid question and you get a stupid answer' is very relevant here. How often, however, do we blame the pupil for the stupid answer instead of ourselves for the stupid question. The most crucial source of information about questions performance is, of course, the pupils themselves, ideally pupils as closely matched as possible to those who will be taking the actual test. It can indeed be the same pupils provided that the teacher has been able to plan a total assessment programme for his or her course. If this has been done then not only will the teachers obtain information which can improve their questions but they can also obtain information which can be used for pupil diagnosis and course evaluation. If pre-testing incidentally is impossible then post-testing, i.e. analysis after use in a real situation is a very valuable second best.

Question analysis

The basic information that analysis can provide in relation to written questions is first, how easy or difficult a question is likely to be in practice (the technical term for this is the facility index); second, how well is it likely to spread out the pupils (the discrimination index); and third, if a multiple-choice objective item is used how satisfactory are all the distractors (option usage). This information, of course, applies to single questions; for the test as a whole the mean and standard deviation already referred to will provide additional information about difficulty and spread. There is, of course, much more that a computer analysis of an objective test could provide but very few readers of this book are ever likely to find it useful or to be called upon to interpret it. Those who are interested in looking further at this topic and are mathematically inclined should consult Nuttall and Willmott, *British Examinations – Techniques of Analysis* to which reference is made in the reading list for this chapter. The calculation of question ease or difficulty when the answer is either right or wrong is a relatively simple matter in the classroom situation. It simply requires a count to be made of those who got the question correct. The result is then divided by the total number in the class and expressed as a fraction or more usually a percentage. With questions involving longer answers this is much less easy but the teacher can get a picture of the relative ease or difficulty of a question by setting down a distribution of the marks gained upon it and relating these to his or her knowledge of the pupils. This is, of course, not quantifiable in the way that is possible for the analysis of the right or wrong answer questions but is none the less useful. There are techniques of analysis for essay questions but these are complex (see Nuttall and Willmott). Calculating the ease or difficulty is one thing, doing something with the information is another. In general questions which are particularly easy or particularly difficult should be avoided. If a complete written test consists of questions which have a facility of between 30 and 70, i.e. they are all answered correctly by between 30 per cent and 70 per cent of those attempting them although it will not, of course, be the same pupils each time, then the test is likely to be of the right difficulty and to give a good spread of marks. What constitutes right difficulty and good spread, however, in the last resort depends upon what these two terms mean to the test constructors and ought to relate to the purpose of the test and the group taking it.

The calculation of a question's discrimination is less easy. What is required is some measure to find out how well a question has spread out the pupils. One can do this most easily in relation to the specific group taking the test in which the question is being used. The discrimination index is thus a measure which tells you whether the best pupils in *this* particular test did better, the same or worse on the question concerned than the worst pupils in this test. The higher the index the better they did, the lower the index the worse they did. It is a reasonable assumption that when a 'best group' does less well on a question than a 'worst group' that there is something wrong with the question but the extent to which the setter of the question wishes it to discriminate will, of course, depend upon the purpose of the test itself.

This verbal description may be made easier for some readers by a practical illustration. This shows how to calculate the facility index (F) and the discrimination index (D) for a multiple-choice item. It can be carried out with relatively small numbers but is better when the numbers exceed 100. It involves no mathematical expertise.

'27' per cent method

The main steps are as follows:

(a) Record the scores of all pupils taking the test in order from high to low, ensuring that each pupil's score is placed opposite his name or number. This can be achieved more simply with small numbers by using the actual scripts or answer books and sorting them into the correct order.

(b) Record or select
   (i) the 27 per cent of the candidates who have obtained the highest scores on the test as a whole,
   (ii) the 27 per cent of the candidates who have obtained the lowest scores on the test as a whole.

In both cases an approximation to the 27 per cent may be made; it is not necessary to be absolutely accurate. 27 per cent has, however, been found to provide the best compromise between, on the one hand, making the extreme groups as large as possible, and, on the other hand, making them as different as possible. In other words, 27 per cent is the optimum value, the use of which enables it to be said with absolute confidence that the selected upper group will be superior in ability to the selected lower group, while at the same time providing an adequate sample upon which to carry out calculations.

(c) Take the answer scripts or mark sheets of the top 27 per cent and record the number of times each option in each multiple-choice item was selected. This information should be placed against the appropriate option upon an actual copy of the test.

(d) Repeat the procedures for the bottom 27 per cent of the pupils. When this has been finished each multiple-choice item in the test will resemble the following example:

(See overleaf)

Making use of the results of assessment

The 1832 Parliamentary Reform Act was important because it

			Top 27 per cent	Bottom 27 per cent
	A	deprived the landed gentry of their influence in Parliament	12	26
48 per cent	B	more than doubled the electorate	3	8
0.44	C	introduced voting by secret ballot	1	6
	<u>D</u>	laid the foundation upon which subsequent Reform Acts were based	38	14
		Omits	0	0

For convenience it is assumed that 200 took the test (27 per cent is therefore 54). The figures in the first column opposite each option gives the number of responses made by the top 27 per cent and the second figure gives the number of responses made by the bottom 27 per cent. At the same time the number of candidates who did not attempt the item (omits) are recorded below as a total figure for both groups.

(e) Take the figures for those in the two groups who selected the correct option D and add them together (in the example given this is 52). Divide this total by the maximum possible sum; that is to say, the number which would have been obtained if *all* candidates in both groups had answered the question correctly (108). Multiply the resultant fraction by 100. The result will be the index of item facility (48 per cent) which, as has been mentioned earlier, can equally well be arrived at by counting the total number of candidates taking the test who answered it correctly and expressing this figure as a percentage.

(f) Subtract the lower group of responses to the correct option from the upper group in this case 14 and 38. Divide the resulting difference (24) by the maximum of the possible difference, which is, of course, the total number of candidates contained in one of the two groups of 27 per cent, in this case 54. The resultant expressed as a decimal fraction is the index of discrimination, in this case 0.44.

Although it is unwise to make definite statements as to what is an appropriate or inappropriate level for item discrimination, given the method of calculation used here we can say that in general terms that a test item with a discrimination index of 0.40 or better discriminates well, while one with an index of between 0.30 and 0.39 is reasonably good. Items with an index of between 0.20 and 0.29 are very marginal and need reviewing, while items with an index of below 0.20 should be rejected. One point should, however, be made here by way of qualification namely that the information provided by these figures relates only to one aspect of the item, namely its ability to discriminate between candidates within the context of the test which is being analysed. It must, therefore, be considered in conjunction with other available information and with the item's relevance and importance in relation to its subject and to the group being tested.

It is not suggested that most teachers will need to undertake such an analysis but it is hoped that its description will serve to underline the importance of ensuring that all questions are of the difficulty and discriminatory power appropriate to their purpose.

Question banking

Questions which have proved themselves to be satisfactory whether the analysis undertaken to determine this has been formal or informal can with advantage be stored together with any information that is available about their performance when used. This not only provides a teacher or group of teachers with a store of proven questions but also enables comparisons to be made about pupil performance over a period of time. If the information resulting from the use of a test composed of questions about which previous data exists differs from previous information then it suggests that the ability of the two groups may be different provided, of course, that the teachers are the same and their teaching strategies have not altered.

The amount of information stored will depend upon the elaborateness of the storage system and the uses to which it is intended to put the bank but the following should be considered: subject matter, kind of question (e.g. multiple-choice, structured, etc.), objective(s) being tested, when and where used, with whom and for what purpose, degree of difficulty and discrimination on each occasion used. A simple card index system can be used at one end of the scale by a single teacher while at the other a computerised retrieval system can be adopted. The advantages of co-operation in the development of a bank between teachers within a single school or between schools is obvious. This is also an area in which public examining boards could aid teachers if they were willing to reconsider changing their current role as purveyors of examinations to one in which they provide consultancy services for teachers seeking to improve the quality of their own assessment within schools and to develop a mixture of internal and external assessment within the external system. The reader interested in exploring the possibilities of question banking further is recommended to consult *Techniques and Problems of Assessment,* ed. Macintosh, Chapter 13. This is referred to in the suggested reading at the end of the book. Chapter 13 itself contains a useful bibliography on the topic.

Conclusion

The contents of this chapter will make no impact upon classroom practice if the majority of teachers maintain their current attitude to statistics, for it is with elementary statistics that this chapter has been concerned. Statistics are not a device to tell teachers what to do or to provide them with information they do not want in a language they do not understand. They are instead a means of enabling them to ask more probing questions about what they are doing, in this case about the assessment they are constructing, and of using the information gained from the answers to improve both their own teaching and their pupils' learning. This is the message of this chapter and if it has not been taken in by the reader then the chapter will have failed, indeed the book itself will have failed, since improving the quality of assessment is but a sterile exercise unless the information it provides is put to use. This requires some understanding of elementary statistics.

Conclusion

The purpose of this book has been to provide teachers in secondary schools with sufficient basic equipment to enable them to appreciate the potential of assessment and to begin to use it to greater advantage within their own school situations. The approach adopted has been limited first, because of the size of the book and second, because the authors believe that it must take account of the actual world in which secondary school teachers currently work, and will continue to work for some time. It is a world in which overemphasis upon cognitive attainment, selection, grading, external examinations, financial stringencies and increasing community demands for accountability will all remain significant factors. In consequence less emphasis has been placed upon the non-cognitive outcomes of education and upon related techniques of measuring them as, for example questionnaires and rating scales, than some might have wished for.

This is not to suggest that assessment in secondary schools ought to remain as restricted in terms of its nature and usage as it is at present. It will so remain, however, if teachers do not wish to use it for a wider range of purposes and in particular do not take advantage of the information that can be gleaned from assessment for diagnosis and evaluation. The suggestions made in this book are intended to provide a platform for such usage. This will only be turned into an adequate base if teachers' present attitudes to assessment change and they are willing to regard it as an essential piece of equipment in their professional armoury instead of something peripheral to be practised at the behest of others or as a downright chore. Until this change occurs the likelihood of adequate provision being made for training in assessment techniques and usage within the present pre- and in-service programmes is a remote one. Teacher control of public examinations will thus remain largely a myth and the possibility of securing fundamental modifications to them and perhaps their ultimate abolition will be correspondingly reduced.

An indication of possible uses for the techniques described in this book will be provided by reference to some proposals put forward and subsequently undertaken by practising teachers following the completion of a week's course in assessment run by the authors. None of the suggestions which are presented exactly as put forward by their proposers are beyond the professional resources of any reader of this book. They may however be beyond the material resources available locally at the present time and it is in relation to follow-up at the local level that most current in-service provision needs attention. Too often what has been learnt on expensive courses is lost upon return to school for want of relatively inexpensive local assistance. Among these proposals were the following:

1 To investigate the most appropriate methods of assessing reading/listening skills in the context of first year Humanities courses with an emphasis upon aural/oral skills;
2 To investigate the predictive value of third year results in Mathematics in respect of external examination performance;
3 To assess the effectiveness of an integrated studies project for first year pupils in a secondary school in terms of changes in the children's attitudes to learning.

All these proposals would of course benefit during their preparation from outside scrutiny in terms of their design and in relation to the quality of the assessment proposed. The organisation of small scale research should indeed form part of any local in-service training programme. They are all, however, manageable and they all deal with practical problems within the proposers' own school for which workable solutions are sought.

The second of the examples given, on the face of it the least elaborate, well illustrates the variety of issues that can emerge from studies such as these. Initially the exercise requires data to be assembled. A three year study may be envisaged in which case what is required are the school's third year results for say 1969, 1970 and 1971 and the examination performances in CSE and GCE O level for 1972, 1973 and 1974. If this data is not available then the study cannot get under way until a two year period has elapsed. The two sets of information can then be correlated on a form basis, a school basis or an individual pupil basis according to the requirements of the design. In the light of the correlations obtained the school might decide to change its existing policies in respect of setting or banding in Mathematics. It might be found that third year results were better predicters of CSE results than of GCE O level or that the results of pupils from some classes predicted better than those from other classes. All these points could be investigated if it were thought useful. The school might decide to undertake a detailed analysis of both its third year examinations and the external examinations in order to see whether they were testing the same things. This might in its turn lead to a reorganisation of some of its Mathematics courses. The possibilities are considerable.

One further illustration taken from a different subject and another school will serve to make this point again. A head of Physics in a school which had roughly 35 pupils a year taking GCE A level Physics undertook a rigorous analysis of his two year Nuffield course and developed over a period of four years a series of multiple-choice objective tests (each test having three parallel forms) designed to measure mastery of the important skills in each unit of the course. These tests were taken by the pupils in their own time following the completion of the relevant unit, using a computer terminal (the teacher worked in co-operation with a colleague who ran the computer studies courses in the school). The tests were scored immediately and the pupils thus received an instant feedback which identified areas of weakness. In the light of these weaknesses they were referred to programmed instructional material designed to remedy them. Apart from the advantages of the scheme in terms of different pacing for different pupils, it also had the merit of encouraging pupils to work on their own, which is an essential component in any preparation for university work. Four years may sound a long time but many teachers devote similar periods to long-term reorganisation of their courses. Had several teachers from different schools been able to co-operate and develop a question bank then the exercise would have taken significantly less time.

The examples given so far are all related as is the majority of this book to cognitive achievements and all make use or propose to make use of the techniques of assessment described in previous chapters. There is no reason however to limit proposals to these areas or these techniques. Following the same course referred to earlier four other participants put forward the following proposals:

1 To formulate a questionnaire in terms of which subject departments might examine and evaluate their own assessment procedures;
2 To investigate how best to communicate school records to various interested groups, i.e. teachers, parents and potential employers;
3 A comparative study of the objectives pursued by subject departments within faculties in a seven faculty academic organisation. The main purposes of the study being to determine to what extent each faculty had or had not common objectives and to formulate a rationale for each of the faculties;
4 To ascertain the objectives of counselling in a secondary school as perceived by members of staff.

These proposals are in many respects much more far-reaching than the first group and would require more assistance in formulation and organisation. In addition to making use of more familiar techniques they would make use

Conclusion

also of questionnaires and rating scales and instruction would need to be provided in these areas.

It is hoped that these examples will have drawn attention, however briefly, to some of the ways in which assessment can be put to practical use in schools other than through the creation of better classroom quizzes or end of term examinations, desirable though improvements here may be. If this together with the basic equipment provided in the earlier chapters does no more than encourage readers to undertake similar exercises in their own schools then it will have achieved its purpose.

Suggestions for further reading

Introduction
MACINTOSH, H. G. and SMITH, L. A., *Towards a Freer Curriculum,* University of London Press, 1974.

Chapter 1
BLOOM, B. S. (ed.), *Taxonomy of Educational Objectives. Handbook 1. The Cognitive Domain.* Longmans, 1956.

BLOOM, B. S., HASTINGS, J. T. and MADAUS, G. F., *Handbook on Formative and Summative Evaluation,* McGraw-Hill, 1971.

COLTHAM, J. B. and FINES, J., 'Educational Objectives for the Study of History', Historical Association Pamphlet TH 35, The Historical Association, 1971.

EBEL, R. L., *Essentials of Educational Measurement,* Prentice-Hall, 1972.

FURST, E. J., *Constructing Evaluation Instruments,* Longman Green, 1958.

GAGNÉ, R. M., *The Conditions of Learning,* Holt, Rinehart & Winston, 1970.

GERLACH, V. S. and SULLIVAN, H. J. in chapter by Sullivan, 'Objectives, evaluation and improved learner achievement' in W. J. Popham (ed.), *Instructional Objectives,* Rand McNally for AERA, Chicago, 1969.

McASHAN, M. M., *Writing Behavioural Objectives. A New Approach,* Harper & Row, 1971.

MAGER, R. F., *Preparing Instructional Objectives,* Fearon, 1962.

POPHAM, W. J., EISNER, E. W., SULLIVAN, H. J. and TYLER, L. L., *Instructional Objectives,* Rand McNally for AERA, 1969.

STONES, E. and ANDERSON, D., *Educational Objectives and the Teaching of Educational Psychology,* Methuen, 1972.

WISEMAN, S. and PIDGEON, D., *Curriculum Evaluation,* NFER, 1970.

WOOD, R., 'Objectives in the teaching of mathematics', *Educational Research* 10, 1968, 83–98.

Suggestions for further reading

Chapter 2

EBEL, R. L., *Essentials of Educational Measurement,* Prentice-Hall, 1972.

EGGLESTON, J. F. and KERR, J. F., *Studies in Assessment,* English Universities Press, 1969.

HUDSON, B. (ed.), *Techniques of Assessment,* Methuen, 1973.

LEWIS, D. G., *Assessment in Education,* University of London Press, 1974.

MACINTOSH, H. G. (ed.), *Techniques and Problems of Assessment,* Edward Arnold, 1974.

MACINTOSH, H. G. and MORRISON, R. B., *Objective Testing,* University of London Press, 1969.

MACINTOSH, H. G. (ed.), *Handbooks on Objective Testing* (16 volumes covering major subjects), Methuen, 1971–4.

PIDGEON, D. and YATES, A., *An Introduction to Educational Measurement,* Routledge & Kegan Paul, 1969.

SCHOFIELD, H., *Assessment and Testing. An Introduction,* Allen & Unwin, 1972.

THYNE, J. M., *Principles of Examining,* University of London Press, 1974.

Chapter 3

The general works referred to in Chapter 2 are equally relevant here.

BLACK, P. J., EGGLESTON, J. F. and MATTHEWS, J. C., *Examining in Advanced Level Science Subjects of the GCE,* Joint Matriculation Board Occasional Publication No. 30, 1970.

FERGUSON, S., *Projects in History,* Batsford, 1967.

HANSON, J. J., *The Use of Resources,* Allen & Unwin, 1975.

HITCHMAN, P. J., *Examining Oral English in Schools,* Methuen, 1966.

OTTER, H. S., *A functional Language Examination,* Oxford Univeristy Press, 1968.

VALETTE, R. M., *Modern Language Testing,* Harcourt Brace & World, 1960.

WILKINSON, A., STRATTA, L. and DUDLEY, P., *The Quality of Listening,* Macmillan, 1974.

Chapter 4

CONTINUA PUBLICATIONS, *Fred Learns Basic Statistics,* 1975.

EBEL, R. L., *Essential of Educational Measurement,* Prentice-Hall, 1972.

GARRETT, H. E., *Statistics in Psychology and Education,* Longmans, 1965.

KLUG, B., *Pro Profiles,* NUS, undated.

LEWIS, D. G., *Statistical Methods in Education,* University of London Press, 1967.

HUDSON, B. (ed.), *Techniques of Assessment,* Methuen, 1973.

MACINTOSH, H. G. (ed.), *Techniques and Problems of Assessment,* Edward Arnold, 1974.

MACINTOSH, H. G. and MORRISON, R. B., *Objective Testing,* University of London Press, 1969.

NUTTALL, D. L. and WILLMOTT, A. S., *British Examinations – Techniques of Analysis,* NFER, 1972.

WOOD, R. and SKURNIK, L. S., *Item Banking,* NFER, 1969.

Conclusion

EVANS, K. M., *Planning Small Scale Research,* NFER, 1968.

NISBET, J. D. and ENTWISTLE, N. J., *Educational Research Methods,* University of London Press, 1970.

OPPENHEIM, A. N., *Questionnaire Design and Attitude Measurement,* Heinemann, 1966.

Students Library of Education

General Editor Lionel Elvin

From College to Classroom: The Probationary Year. Derek Hanson and Margaret Herrington. 128 pp.
The Study of Education. J. W. Tibble. 240 pp.

METHOD

Change in Art Education. Dick Field. 132 pp.
Changing Aims in Religious Education. Edwin Cox. 108 pp.
Children and Learning to Read. Elizabeth J. Goodacre. 128 pp.
Discovery Learning in the Primary School. John Foster. 158 pp.
Environmental Studies. D. G. Watts. 128 pp.
*The Future of the Sixth Form.** A. D. C. Peterson. 96 pp.
*Inspecting and the Inspectorate.** John Blackie. 112 pp.
*The Learning of History.** D. G. Watts. 128 pp.
*The Middle School Experiment.** Reese Edwards. 112 pp.
Reading in Primary Schools. Geoffrey R. Roberts. 108 pp.
Spelling: Caught or Taught? Margaret L. Peters. 96 pp.
Students into Teachers: Experiences of Probationers in Schools. Mildred Collins. 112 pp.

HISTORY

*Advisory Councils and Committees in Education.** Maurice Kogan and Tim Packwood. 136 pp.
The American Influence on English Education. W. H. G. Armytage. 128 pp.
The Changing Sixth Form in the Twentieth Century. A. D. Edwards. 115 pp.
*Church, State and Schools in Britain 1800–1970.** James Murphy. 192 pp.
*English Education and the Radicals 1780–1850.** Harold Silver. 148 pp.
*English Primary Education and the Progressives 1914–1939.** R. J. W. Selleck. 206 pp.
The Evolution of the Comprehensive School 1926–1972. David Rubinstein and Brian Simon. 148 pp.
The Evolution of the Nursery-Infant School. Nanette Whitbread. 160 pp.

The Foundations of Twentieth-Century Education. E. Eaglesham. 128 pp.

The French Influence on English Education. W. H. G. Armytage. 128 pp.

*The German Influence on English Education. W. H. G. Armytage. 142 pp.

Mediaeval Education and the Reformation. J. Lawson. 128 pp.

Recent Education from Local Sources. Malcolm Seaborne. 128 pp.

*The Russian Influence on English Education. W. H. G. Armytage. 138 pp.

Secondary School Reorganization in England and Wales. Alun Griffiths. 128 pp.

Social Change and the Schools: 1918–1944. Gerald Bernbaum. 128 pp.

The Social Origins of English Education. Joan Simon. 132 pp.

PHILOSOPHY

Education and the Concept of Mental Health. John Wilson. 99 pp.

Indoctrination and Education. I. A. Snook. 128 pp.

Interest and Discipline in Education. P. S. Wilson. 142 pp.

The Logic of Education. P. H. Hirst and R. S. Peters. 196 pp.

Philosophy and the Teacher. Edited by D. I. Lloyd. 180 pp.

The Philosophy of Primary Education. R. F. Dearden. 208 pp.

Plato and Education. Robin Barrow. 96 pp.

Problems in Primary Education. R. F. Dearden. 160 pp.

PSYCHOLOGY

Creativity and Education. Hugh Lytton. 144 pp.

Group Study for Teachers. Elizabeth Richardson. 144 pp.

Human Learning: A Developmental Analysis. H. S. N. McFarland. 136 pp.

An Introduction to Educational Measurement. D. Pidgeon and A. Yates. 122 pp.

Modern Educational Psychology: An Historical Introduction. E. G. S. Evans. 118 pp.

An Outline of Piaget's Developmental Psychology. Ruth M. Beard. 144 pp.

Personality, Learning and Teaching. George D. Handley. 126 pp.

*Teacher Expectations and Pupil Learning. Roy Nash. 128 pp.

Teacher and Pupil: Some Socio-Psychological Aspects. Philip Gammage. 128 pp.

Troublesome Children in Class. Irene E. Caspari. 160 pp.

SOCIOLOGY

Basic Readings in the Sociology of Education. D. F. Swift. 368 pp.

Class, Culture and the Curriculum. Denis Lawton. 140 pp.

Culture, Industrialisation and Education. G. H. Bantock. 108 pp.

*__Education at Home and Abroad.__ Joseph Lauwerys and Graham Tayar. 144 pp.

Education, Work and Leisure. Harold Entwistle. 118 pp.

The Organization of Schooling: A Study of Educational Grouping Practices. Alfred Yates. 116 pp.

*__Political Education in a Democracy.__ Harold Entwistle. 144 pp.

The Role of the Pupil. Barbara Calvert. 160 pp.

The Role of the Teacher. Eric Hoyle. 112 pp.

The Social Context of the School. S. John Eggleston. 128 pp.

The Sociology of Educational Ideas. Julia Evetts. 176 pp.

CURRICULUM STUDIES

*__Towards a Compulsory Curriculum.__ J. P. White. 122 pp.

INTERDISCIPLINARY STUDIES

*__Educational Theory: An Introduction.__ T. W. Moore. 116 pp.

Perspectives on Plowden. R. S. Peters. 116 pp.

*__The Role of the Head.__ Edited by R. S. Peters. 136 pp.

* Library edition only